CROSSING THE PLAINS IN 1852

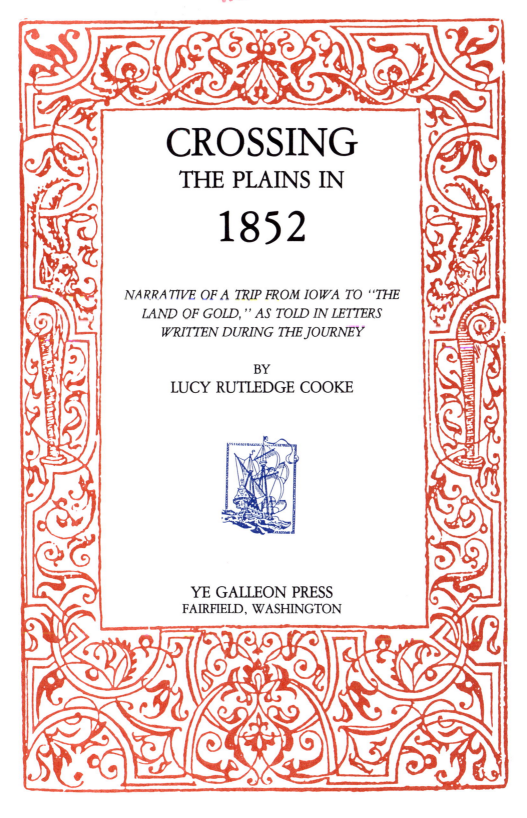

CROSSING
THE PLAINS IN
1852

*NARRATIVE OF A TRIP FROM IOWA TO "THE
LAND OF GOLD," AS TOLD IN LETTERS
WRITTEN DURING THE JOURNEY*

BY
LUCY RUTLEDGE COOKE

YE GALLEON PRESS
FAIRFIELD, WASHINGTON

PRINTED SOLELY FOR THE DESCENDANTS OF THE AUTHOR
IN MEMORY OF THE FAITH AND OPTIMISM THAT
WERE HERS THROUGHOUT THE PERILOUS
JOURNEY OF THOSE EARLY DAYS
"ACROSS THE PLAINS."

ISBN 0-87770-430-9

Library of Congress Cataloging in Publication Data

Cooke, Lucy Rutledge, 1827-1915.
 Crossing the plains in 1852: narrative of a trip from Iowa to "The Land
of Gold," as told in letters written during the journey / by Lucy Rutledge
Cooke.

 p. cm.
 Overland journeys to the Pacific. 2. West (U.S.) — Description and
travel — 1848-1860. 3. California — Description and travel — 1848-1869.
4. Cooke, Lucy Rutledge, 1827-1915 — Correspondence. 5. California Trail.
6. Pioneers — West (U.S.) — Correspondence. I. Title.

F593.C73   1987   917.8'042   [B]   87-27903
ISBN 0-87770-430-9

FOREWORD

Virginia City, Nevada, March, 1895.

THE ACCOMPANYING LETTERS ARE COPIES FROM the original written by me in journalistic style while crossing the plains in 1852-53, enroute to California. They were written to my dear sister, Mrs. Willis, who was then living on their farm at Rockingham, near Davenport, Scott county, Iowa. She preserved my communications, and when on a visit to us in Dutch Flat, Placer county, California (where we lived for nineteen years), in 1874, she returned my letters to me, which gave us much pleasure, as we could then read and recall so many of the incidents therein narrated.

They have all been preserved and are much valued, and will, if not destroyed by fire, eventually belong to my eldest girl, Sarah (Mrs. Lane).

To please an oft request of my third daughter, Genevieve, or ''Gen'' as she is called at home, I have promised to make a copy in this book of those letters, and anticipate much pleasure in so doing.

5

I think perhaps it would be best to explain our respective situations, so more fully to enter into our circumstances at the time this great journey was undertaken.

The "California Gold Fever" broke out in 1849. I was married on December 26th of that year, and can well remember the excitement of all, young and old, at the desire to start for the "Land of Gold," and daily during the summer do I remember seeing the white canvas-topped wagons slowly wending their way along the banks of the Mississippi on either shore (Illinois or Iowa), with their eager occupants en route for Council Bluffs, the general rendevous or gathering place for all "California bound." We were then living at Moline, Illinois, on the banks of the Mississippi. My sister lived on the Iowa side; but we frequently visited back and forth, crossing on the ferry boat plying between Rock Island and Davenport.

My uncle, William Rutledge, who was a Baptist minister, lived at Le Claire, a small town in Iowa at the head of the rapids, sixteen miles above Davenport. He and family and my sister were my only relatives until I was married. We left Moline in the spring of 1851 to join Mrs. Cooke Sr., who was then living in Dubuque, Iowa, teaching vocal and instrumental music. She had a large patronage, and with my husband I assisted in several of her concerts. We remained here over a year, during which time my Sarah was born, August 16, 1851.

In the spring of 1852, the "California fever" being still at "fever heat," we were enthused to try our fortunes with the crowds going.

So everything was sold off and wagons and teams purchased preparatory to the journey.

Mr. Cooke, my husband's father, secured twelve young men as passengers, who paid their fare to be delivered in Sacramento, California, so those, with our own family, consisting of ten persons, including myself and baby, made a goodly company. We started from Dubuque with four wagons, one a light spring drawn by two horses, the others having oxen with cows for "leaders."

Mr. Cooke started his men folks first, to drive across Iowa to Council Bluffs on the western side of the state, whilst Mrs. Cooke, two young children, myself and baby, were driven by Mr. Cooke Sr. down to Davenport in our two-horse wagon with covered top and laden to the bows. We wished to bid farewell to remaining friends ere we started the "Plains across." I spent my brief sojourn with my sister and her husband at Rockingham; then Mr. Cooke Sr. took our team and joined the company at the Bluffs, leaving Mrs. Cooke, myself and children to come down the river on the steamboat plying to St. Louis, and thence up the Missouri River to our destination, where our company would be awaiting us.

Thus I have briefly sketched our plans and goings till the time we reached St. Louis, from which place my first letter is written. My dear uncle had gone to England the year before, and returned just as we started our journey. I did not see the dear face again, though but for some mistake we might have met to say farewell, as he had arrived home again.

LUCY RUTLEDGE COOKE.

LETTER NUMBER ONE.

On board Boat Pontiac No. 2, St. Louis, Mo., April 15, 1852.

DEAREST SISTER MARIANNE: I MET WITH FRIENDS, Mr. and Mrs. Belcher of Le Claire, on board the boat *Golden Era,* who informed me that Uncle returned the Sunday before I started down the river. It was a great pity some of the family could not have come down on the Monday before I left. I could then have seen them and heard about our friends in England from Uncle. I wrote a letter to him and gave it to one of the Le Claire folks who was aboard. We arrived here last eve (Wednesday) before supper, having been only one night coming down the river. We did not see "John Richards" at the landing, as expected, therefore we stayed on board another night, and this morning (Thursday) Ma went to hunt him up and succeeded in finding him, and we have now taken our passage on this boat to go up the Missouri. Will you not think the rate of passage enormously high, $70 for our passage, $20 for each passenger; though John R. will assist to wait on table, for which service the captain deducts $10 from his fare.

The boat is laden with people bound for California, and their outfits, teams, etc., and indeed so is all St. Louis filled with them, and you would be amused could you look down in this cabin and see the tables full of young men writing their last letters to friends ere we start up this river.

But oh, I fear we shall have a terrible time, for there seems to be thousands going. But some are returning from the Bluffs (Council) giving up the idea when they see the crowds, thus fearing disaster at the very start. I could almost wish William and I were of their number. Poor Ma said only this morning, "Oh, I wish we never had started," and she looks so sorrowful and dejected. I think if Pa had not passengers to take through she would urge him to return; not that he would be so inclined for returning is hopeless.

There are some very pleasant ladies on board, who like ourselves are going to the Bluffs to join their husbands and friends, so I anticipate pleasant company. There is also a company of fifty young men on board from Cinncinnati.

The *Dr. Franklin No. 2* did not go up the Missouri as advertised. Ma was talking of it to a gent on the *Golden Era*; he said she would be sure not to run up there, as she was only insured for the Mississippi; and when we arrived at St. Louis she was just starting back for Dubuque, so had we come down on her we must have changed boats at this place.

This boat they say will start tonight, but that may be only talk; but the weather is so pleasant I enjoy the boat, and don't care when we leave. There is an English lady here quite busy knitting fancy white stockings—such a pretty pattern; she will show me all about mine. That is nice!

Though we have been on board but a few hours, we seem well acquainted already. Each Californian treats another as old acquaintances, and all are so agreeable. One lady now is walking up and down with my baby while I am writing this. The stewardess is English, from James street, near Oxford street, right at our old home! She has traveled considerably. Her father was in the Hudson's Bay Company, and she went with him. She seems very fond of babies, so doubtless will accommodate me when I have baby's washing to do. The stewardess on the *Golden Era* was awfully crabbed and unaccommodating in that way, which was very inconvenient to me.

But I must hasten, or the lady will tire of caring for baby. Tell Mrs. Wright I adopted her plan of giving baby to her because she said, "Oh, what a sweet baby," and if all held her who praise her I shall scarce be able to nurse her the whole distance, for everyone says; "What a sweet, healthy-looking child she is." Give my kindest regards to Mrs. Wright and Sarah and all the Colmans.

We have just dined. Had nice lettuce, spring onions, rhubarb and asparagus, and really the weather seems hot. The waiters are all in shirt sleeves. The California-bound men look a motley group. Some have oilcloth coats and hats, and near all wear hickory shirts. I dined in my brown gingham dress, thinking I should even then look well as the rest.

The Moline folks were not on the boat with us, as they did not hail the boat, and so it passed without calling at Moline. But we may meet them before we start. I fear I shall not hear from you any more until we arrive in California. However, I shall write from Council Bluffs, and often after as there's a chance. Direct to us at Sacramento City, care of "Gratiot & Childs." My side still troubles me, though perhaps it's a little better; my ankle is still weak. Baby is well. I think we shall not need cloaks again.

Kindest love to yourself and your dear husband. Good bye. Lovingly yours ever,   LUCY.

The men passengers are trying their guns, and there is such a noise.

LETTER NUMBER TWO.

On board Boat Pontiac No. 2, Missouri River, April 19, 1852.

DEAREST MARIANNE: BEING QUITE UNOCCUPIED, I sit me down to write a little account of journey thus far. This is Monday eve. We came on board last Friday morn, and at present have only come about 200 miles! Oh, what tedious traveling it is on this river. Our boat is a very slow one, and is very heavily laden. But it's discouraging to know we have not come one-fourth of the distance. The river abounds with sandbars, on which we sometimes ''stick'' for hours. Last night we were on one most of the night. Methinks it's well, dear Polly, it is not you traveling thus, for you would be scared all the time, for the river abounds with floating logs and snags; it seems a wonder the boat should run at night.

Yesterday was the Sabbath. How I should enjoy riding with you and your dear husband to Davenport, and hear that good man, Mr. Adams, preach. But that is all past as a ''tale that is told.'' We had some hymn-singing on board, and it rejoiced my heart to look over the guards down to the deck and see a company of men singing from hymn books, and then engage in reading a portion of Scripture.

13

We stopped to "wood up" within four miles of town, and so many of the men got off and walked to the town; and there came again on board. The men rush down every time the boat stops, as though we had been at sea for a month. Today we passed Jefferson City, the capital of Missouri. There is a splendid state house on the banks of the river. We have not as yet passed more than three or four towns, so we see nothing to interest us. We passed a few orchards; the trees were so covered with blossoms. Oh, how it made me think of your happy and pleasant home in Rockingham. Ma is just as downcast as ever; thinks we shall never be happy again! Today she said she would be willing to teach a class of piano scholars a year gratis, could she be back in Dubuque as comfortably fixed as she was before we started. She says no argument used to induce her to leave there seems to have any weight now. I think she would have me believe it was entirely on William's account they have made this move. But I cannot quite agree to that, for her other sons' good had equal weight.

Oh, I do long to reach the Bluffs, to see if our husbands are in good spirits about the journey.

My dear babe was vaccinated from Richard W. It was only done in one place, but it has "taken" nicely, so I'm glad only one scar is made. Richard had three, and his arm was terribly inflamed. Tell Mrs. Wright Ma is afraid to use cold water at such a time. Richard's arm was in such inflammation, and she kept putting on cold wet cloths all one night. Dear baby is so good; she goes to sleep now in the eve without crying, and takes a sleep of two or three hours each morning. John R. seems so attached to her, and takes charge of her each meal time, so I eat in comfort at first table. I bought her a little wicker chair in St. Louis, with a little table in front for her playthings; gave $1.50 for it. She likes it very much. I have not padded it yet; don't know if I shall. I get along pretty well with baby's washing as there's a good place for drying outside.

At first we had a double stateroom in the gentlemen's cabin, which was very uncomfortable, but it is now exchanged for one in the ladies' cabin, which we find more convenient. My side sometimes is very painful. I have not applied mustard. I don't seem to have opportunity to attend to myself.

Tuesday. Dear baby slept all afternoon whilst I sewed. After dinner I did her washing whilst one of the ladies took care of her; had quite a washing—aprons, nightgowns, petticoats, etc. My ankle was very troublesome when I first came on board. One of the passengers wished me to melt some beeswax and tallow and make a plaster.

How very much colder it seems as we go up the river; there's but little appearance of spring. I wonder how Mr. Willis gets along with his plowing. Oh, how long it seems since I have seen my dear husband. I have written once since we left St. Louis. Suppose it will reach him before I do. We are doubtful where this boat will take us, for saying we want to go to Council Bluffs it seems is rather indefinite, as they extend over two hundred miles. Some say we shall not go higher than "St. Jo." But I trust all will come out right Lilly has just been hemming four silk handkerchiefs for a gent who gave her fifty cents for so doing. The lady passengers are at a loss to know how to amuse themselves. I wonder what we shall find to do before we reach our journey's end. I have only dressed baby in her pretty red sacque twice. I don't like her to wear it, fearing its beauty will soon be spoiled. Ma admires it so much.

Thursday afternoon, April 22d. Dear Sister: My little babe is so sick. I was up all night with her. She takes little or no nourishment, and what she does, cannot retain. She moans all the time, and is in high fever. We think perhaps it comes of her vaccination. At first we thought it whooping cough coming on, as she coughed very much. I have also been very poorly; kept my bed most of the day yesterday. I intend to mail this at Lexington, where

15

we expect to be in an hour. We shall then be fifty miles short of half way. Oh, how I wish we never had started for the Golden Land. But I must bid you and your dear husband adieu. I shall write whenever there is opportunity. Why "they say" this is the 22d. Is it not your birthday? God bless you, my beloved sister, and I fervently pray we may each be spared to meet again in this world. But if not—let us strive to spend together a blissful eternity!

How surprised you would be should we return from the "Bluffs." I wish there was a chance of it.

Yours ever affectionately,   LUCY.

LETTER NUMBER THREE.

On board the Robert Campbell, on the Missouri, April 30, 1852.

DEAREST SISTER: MY LAST LETTER TO YOU WAS sealed and ready for mailing before we arrived at Lexington, at which place a passenger took it ashore. When we arrived there the boat stopped alongside of a wreck of a boat that had been blown up two weeks previous, the *Saluda*. Never shall I forget the sight it presented, even two weeks after. There was not the width of two planks in any part of the boat; boilers and everything gone, just the skeleton left. The machinery was lying around on the banks. Two or three houses were also blown down by the explosion, Doubtless many of the passengers, like ourselves, were on their way to their friends. The boat had just made the landing. Not one had gone ashore, so most of the passengers were instantly killed. But strange to tell, not one cabin boy was hurt. John R. knew most of them.

But now we have our disasters to record, and this long-to-be-remembered Missouri has another. We arrived at Weston on Sunday afternoon (25th) on board *Pontiac No. 2*. Took on a few passengers. Proceeded slowly till Monday morning, when about nine o'clock we saw men running and crying ''Man overboard!''

17

But it was presently hushed up, and we saw gents laughing, which soon allayed our fears. But in about half an hour I saw deck hands and cabin boys running into the staterooms gathering blankets and comforters. We were then informed we had run across a log on a "sandbar" and had stove a hole in the bottom of the boat, and they were trying to stop the hole with bedding. But it failed, so in ten or fifteen minutes we were passengers on a sunken boat. But fortunately the water was shallow, so we were only submerged about three feet. Still, we seemed to be sinking lower and lower.

The clerk (who owned the boat) came into the ladies' cabin much agitated, and told the ladies to put on their bonnets and shawls with as much haste as possible. But I cannot say any of us seemed much alarmed. Still, all was confusion, and to add to our discomfort it was a very cold, windy morning, and had just commenced to rain. We were about 150 feet from shore. Well, a colored man took baby, whilst I carried my carpet bag, and down to the front of the boat we hurried. When we arrived there the boat had so settled that water was up over the deck. So we had to walk on raised planks. But we were too late to get in the first yawl load, it being already full, and we were hurried back to the ladies' cabin, being assured we should be safe and more comfortable than ashore, there being only one little old cabin in sight. We therefore kept pretty contented for about an hour, when the boat gave signs of breaking in two. It was therefore again thought advisable to put us ashore. So to the yawl again we went, and after a big struggle in the crowd, managed to get in; but the yawl was crowded, as each passenger was anxious to set foot on terra firma. The river was very rough, and it took four men to row. However, we were soon ashore, and could then have a good view of the *Pontiac* in her disabled condition, and reflect on our own situation.

We landed among timber, so the men immediately set fire to a felled tree, and we soon had a famous blaze, and as more passengers came ashore more fires were kindled. Still, the ground was very damp and covered with dead leaves and timber. Ma advised me to go with baby to the lone cabin, which I did, but found its only room already full. But I sat down awhile, and then, feeling very hungry, it being noon, I went back to the folks, and then found they had all had their dinners, as provisions had been sent over from the boat for the cabin passengers.

I was somewhat vexed with my folks for not thinking of or saving food for me, as there was none then left. But this only brought reproof from Ma (with a full stomach), and she chided me for showing temper on such an occasion. But my stomach was empty and I had my baby to nurse. I was told there was a house about half a mile distant, where several had been and got dinner. So off I posted with my baby and found a pretty comfortable dwelling in the woods, with the dinner table set. So I made quick despatch of biscuits, butter and molasses, with three or four cups of tea, after which I felt considerably better tempered.

I sat down to the fire, and in my lonely condition how I longed for my dear husband, who was then so ignorant of my situation. I expected possibly we might have to remain there a day or two before another boat might arrive. But in an hour or so we heard a boat was in sight so I quickly gathered my "traps." A gent kindly took baby, and back to our landing place we started. When we arrived there we found this new captain refused to charter his boat alongside of the sunken vessel, without which it was illegal to do so, and besides, not any of our baggage had been put ashore. So it was useless for the passengers to leave the sunken boat. However, some few of them went on with her and left us to our fate, though two other boats were on their way, and that news greatly cheered us all. It was not till dusk we secured our baggage, there being but the one yawl to convey back and forth, and John R. had almost to fight his way in getting all our things. "Each for himself" was the general rule.

As it was now near dark, the cabin boys and cook brought ashore cooking utensils and food preparatory for a supper. So just as the moon was rising we were seated in front of a large tray filled with cold meats, coffee, hard crackers, etc., and all seemed to eat with considerable relish. We had brilliant fires, and the scene was weird, though perhaps quite fitting for such a company of prospective Californians. I, however, felt the effects of sitting on the damp ground. My knees trembled so I could not sit still, and I was fearful baby would suffer, and there was no shelter for any.

At this juncture a boat came up the river, and as we had our baggage with us, only carpet bags (our chief things having gone overland in our wagons with Pa), we obtained our passage on this boat, the Midas, and toward midnight we went aboard.

It was a lovely moonlight night, but the bright moon looked dim compared to our numerous fires on shore. The Midas laid by till morning and then took on more passengers and baggage, few being so fortunate as ourselves in not losing anything on board the Pontiac.

The Midas at length left the ill-fated boat and those of the passengers who were trying to get their baggage which happened to be on deck, all that in the hold being a total loss. The boat was then nine feet under water at her bows, and four and a-half feet at stern. She was broken across where she laid across the log. The captain refused to refund any of the passage money to the ''Bluffs,'' and would not allow any person to bring baggage ashore without paying heavily for it. One gent was taxed $100 for his team, himself and other men, and then had to pay $6 for getting a barrel ashore. The men worked all night getting what they could from the boat. There were many wagons on the ''hurricane deck;'' all, however, were safely landed by morning. There were many horses and mules, and poor creatures they stood for hours up to their knees in water, then were cut loose, and a man in the yawl dragged one, at which the others followed to shore. But we were now on the Midas, and so left our late fellow-passengers to their fate.

We reached St. Joseph, or "St. Jo," about eleven o'clock Tuesday morning, and there had to engage passage in other boats for the "Bluffs," as the Midas went no higher. St. Jo looked all astir with Californians. We thought possibly some of our men folks might be there. There were four boats there. On one was a band of music. The players struck up for our edification "Home, Sweet Home." This seemed scarce appropriate, as many if not most were leaving their "homes." But presently they changed to

Oh, Susannah, don't you cry for me,
I'm bound for California,
The gold dust for to see."

This lively strain seemed to affect all and put them on the "jig."

We were fortunate in having paid the captain of the Pontiac only $36, as he would have refunded none. The Midas took us to St. Jo for two dollars each. We, however, have left that boat, and are now on the one that first passed us when our boat had sunken. She did not leave St. Louis for three days after we had, so you can judge of our rate of travel. Well, we seemed to stick on sandbars every few hours. We reckoned to reach the "Bluffs" in three days, but the first night on board we "stuck" for eighteen hours. Then after that we got along pretty well till yesterday, when we "stuck" again six hours. The lead was thrown for soundings. I sat and watched them a long time. First they cried, "twelve and a half feet." But it soon got down (or up) to "three feet scarce," and there we stuck, as this boat draws three and a half feet. Then all the men passengers and horses were put ashore to walk about a mile and so lightened the boat, and so after a while she managed to get over the bar.

We often see Indians, one of whom directed the pilot where the channel was, and found it as the Indian said. Last night we laid by, the wind being too high, and all night it blew in hurricanes. The captain came at midnight to tell the chambermaid to dress and see if the ladies were scared. I was sleeping on the cabin floor, but I was not troubled, for we seemed to have had so many disasters I was getting used to it. So I soon was fast asleep again.

It is now about three in the afternoon, and we are still chained to a tree on the bank, the wind being too high to try further. We are only about sixty miles from the ''Bluffs'' and this morning the horses were put ashore to go afoot, and likely they may reach our destination ere we do. We sent a letter to our folks telling of our misfortunes, and now if no more ill luck befalls us could soon be with them.

It is two weeks today since we left St. Louis. I shall now quit writing till we reach the ''Bluffs,'' and do hope there will be a letter awaiting from you.

Good bye, dearest Marianne.

————

Wednesday Morning, May 5, 1852. Here I am, seated in our spring wagon, with baby stretched out at my feet asleep. We arrived at Kanesville last Saturday (May 1st). We hoped to see our folks soon as the boat landed, but were disappointed. The town lies four miles back from the river. We went up on the hurricane deck and sat there, wondering what we should do, when Ma happened to see in the crowd an old gent from Dubuque. She called to him and inquired about our folks. He knew all about them, and said some of them would soon be down at the landing, as from the town they could see when a boat arrived.

Well, in about an hour or two, William, Pa, Thomas and Eddie arrived in a four-horse wagon. They had not till then heard of our disasters on the *Pontiac*, but had been expecting us on it for days. You may be sure we had a joyful meeting. All seemed well and perfectly happy with regard to the trip before us.

Pa found an engagement in a store here soon as he arrived with his teams, at $50 a month salary. Well, they drove us all "home" in great glee. Ma stopped at the Methodist minister's house with the little children, and William and I went to a cabin which Mr. Rickey (a Dubuque neighbor of ours) was occupying. We slept on our robes on the floor, and laid and laughed as we looked through the holes in the roof to the sky. The cabin was not so tight as Mr. Willis' barn, and I felt the wind blow in terribly. But who cared? Not I.

On Sunday, May 2d, we all went to church, but I had to leave before close of sermon, as baby was so fussy. In the evening William got the tent ready for us to occupy, so I took up my abode there. It is such a fine tent, and so large. Pa bought it here for $10. It is a government tent, second hand, but very strong. The one we made is used by our men folks. William and I have slept in the light wagon lately, as Ma came to the tent, and we preferred a place to ourselves. But it's very crowded in the wagon, and I have to lay baby across our heads. But still we'll try to make it answer.

You will expect me to write something of the California emigration here. Well, there are not nearly so many teams camped around as I expected to find. But they say more than half that were here are now gone out, but fresh ones are coming all the time, giving the town an appearance of a country fair. This Kanesville is a poor little mean place. I don't think there's a brick house in it. Most of the dwellings are log cabins. We move out tomorrow (May

6th) and drive to the bottom about ten miles off, where there is a ferry across the river (Missouri). We expect to camp here about a week previous to our final start, as the grass is hardly forward enough yet for stock. All the Dubuque company will camp there and then start together. William has just sold that span of horses we came to your house with. He thought one of them was not strong enough for our trip. They were sold at auction for $165, without harness. William is going to buy three more yoke of oxen. One of our cows calved yesterday. How I did wish you could have had the calf, as our folks will kill it or give it to the Indians.

We gave a concert last night, Ma always having an eye to business. It was a mean kind of hall, the platform so broken I fell through when I went to sit down on my chair. But we all laughed together and thought it all in keeping with the surroundings. Ma, William, John and I were the performers. We knew lots of popular songs and negro melodies, which took the audience, and they generously applauded everything. I played duets with Ma. The house was crowded, though it was but small. Our costumes were the ones we were to travel in. We borrowed a piano in town, our own team hauling it. Well, after expenses were paid we had $25, so that will pay some ferriages, and it was worth our trouble, and we always enjoy singing together.

Thomas and another young fellow do our cooking. We have two little sheetiron stoves. I would prefer cooking for myself and William, as the boys keep everything so dirty, but fortunately I am always hungry, so don't notice dirt. Ma proposed for she and I to take turns cooking for our own family, and let John and the young man cook for the men. But John would not consent to do a part, as he needed both stoves at a time when we should be needing one.

Friday night, May 7th. Well, here we are at rest again. We left Kanesville this morning, and have come about eight miles today, and expect to cross the river some time tomorrow, our tickets coming in turn then. We are now camped on a large bottom, surrounded by magnificent bluffs, at the base of one of which we have spread our tents. We reached here in good time today, suppose about one o'clock. There were not many teams in then, so we had our pick of camping ground. And oh, lovely is the view! Many of the men climbed one of the steepest bluffs at back of our tents. They took a drum and fife, etc., and what a noise they did make. Then they all marched down in procession.

There are now, I should judge, seventy or eighty wagons around here, so we have plenty of company, and all are busy with their outfits. In our men's tent just now they are playing violin, banjo and bones, and the noise has attracted a crowd. Each tries to give his help to the din. And then the frogs! Well, they are heard above it all.

When we arrived here today our men turned all our cattle loose to feed, and just before dark were collecting them again, tying them to stakes ready for our start next morning. But they found two cows were missing, and now are gone back to Kanesville to hunt them. One of the missing cows is the one which just had a calf. I wonder none of them thought she would go back to it if given a chance, and so have tied her up. William sold the calf for fifty cents to a man, and presently a boy came along with a calf, and one of our men, not knowing our calf was disposed of, told the boy to come to our tent and he should have it. So he came and took it away. Well, in about an hour along came the rightful owner. Then there was trouble, as his calf was gone. So he left, with terrible big words; said he would "go for it," and the smartest should win.

Wednesday evening we had a storm. The rain came down in torrents, and continued nearly all night. Oh, what a miserable plight we were in, for our folks had not dug any trench around our tent. So as we were on the side of the bluff the rain soon ran in, and not a dry spot did we have. Unfortunately our little wagon in

25

which William and I slept was in town at the blacksmith's, so we had to sleep on the ground for the first time. But we had two heavy bolsters and several pillows under us. Ma had a straw bed. Mr. Rickey's folks had moved out of the cabin they rented near by, so William went and made a big fire in the fireplace, thinking we might as well occupy it. He then came for us to go over to it. But when he returned to the cabin with our bedding he found it full of Indians, apparently well pleased with their warm quarters. Oh, but William was mad at his trouble of making a fire at night, and he scolded me because I refused to go and have him turn the Indians out. But I did not fancy the place to sleep in after they had been there. So we let them remain in the warm shelter, and we did the best we could.

In the morning everything was wet, still we had to pack up and move on, so as to be near the ferry. But the rain poured down, and we waited another day. The sun came out, so I hung our bedding and clothing out to dry, and thus make us comfortable for an early start next morning.

I am pleased to tell you Mr. Gilbert, whom we used to board with at Moline, came into Kanesville on Wednesday. He went into a store there and heard some one say "Mr. Cooke," and looking around saw Pa there, and from him learned where we were. He came immediately to our tent, and was so glad to meet us again. We talked over matters, and soon decided to travel in company if possible.

We are now camped four miles from the ferry, but suppose we shall meet Mr. Gilbert there tomorrow, as our turn to cross comes before his. Pa will quit the store tomorrow.

Saturday, May 8th. I am sorry to find this is my last chance to write for some time, and I am so disappointed that no letter from you has reached me here. I feel certain you sent by the Newby's, who have not yet arrived. But doubtless they soon will overtake us, and then if they bring me a budget what pleasure it will give me. Pa bought us a nice pair of waterproof blankets to put on the ground under our bedding, so now when it rains we'll do better.

William complains very much of the quantity of baggage Ma and I have, as it has all to be moved night and morning. I had a cry about it this morning, as I seemed to have parted with near every article I valued, as having brought it from London but a short time ago, and the memories were still very dear. When William saw me crying, he promised never more to complain of my possessions, and that henceforth it would be his chief delight to "tote" my things back and forth. Then we both kissed and made up, and were happy again.

Our three heavy wagons seem full to top of bows, containing food, clothing, bedding, etc., of our passengers as also our own family's, though our wagon has our bedding and a small box of mine, baby's little wicker chair, and sundry other things. We have steps at the back so we can get in and out easily. We rode very comfortably yesterday from Kanesville. Baby sat in her chair most of the time whilst Ma and I sewed. Yes, sewed! Don't laugh. I made Sis a little sunbonnet.

Soon after we camped here a farm wagon came up with corn, hay, butter, chickens and eggs for sale. We bought four chickens at 12½ cents each, and had them for supper tonight; they were so nice. Provisions are quite reasonable at Kanesville. Fine potatoes, 40 and 45 cents a bushel, corn 25 cents, eggs 6 cents. Flour is dear now. $10 per barrel. Pa bought 36 pounds of prunes, two big boxes of figs, and a nice lot of raisins, so we (ourselves) can have a little treat occasionally.

Saturday. A gent has just come for our letters to mail, so I hastily close, but could tell lots more. Shall try to write from Fort Laramie. Give lots of love to dear Mr. Willis. Yours lovingly,

May 8, 1852   SISTER LUCY.

It was at Kanesville, Iowa, that the Dubuque Emigrating Company was formed, of which the following is the record preserved by the writer of these letters:

BY-LAWS AND RESOLUTIONS

OF THE

DUBUQUE EMIGRATING COMPANY
TO CALIFORNIA

———

Adopted April, 1852
Kanesville, Iowa
Printed at the Western Bugle Office

Adopted at a meeting held in Kanesville, Iowa, April 29, 1852, at which Colonel George Madeira was called to preside, and Mr. William Cooke acted as secretary.

1st: The general organization shall be composed of divisions of not less than ten nor more than twenty-five teams, each one of which shall choose its own officers, which shall consist of a captain and secretary, who shall be elected every Saturday night at the call of the existing secretary, a majority of votes electing.

2d: It shall be the duty of the captain to take a general supervision of his own company, and to act in concert with each other in inspecting the outfits before starting, and in selecting the most practicable routes, crossings of streams and camping grounds, and to give the orders for stopping and starting.

3d: It shall be the duty of each secretary to keep a record of all the names of individuals in his company, also a list of every able-bodied male member liable to stand of guard, and to call the guard to duty each night according to their turn on the roll.

4th: Every male member of the company over sixteen years of age shall be liable to perform duty on guard at night when not disqualified by sickness.

Resolved: First—That we will not receive into our organization any company or person without suitable outfit for the journey.

Second—That we will observe the Christian Sabbath and attend religious service whenever practicable.

Third—That we will avoid open immorality of every kind, such as profane swearing, gambling, and the use of intoxicating drinks as a beverage.

Fourth—That we will render mutual assistance to each member of the organization in cases of sickness or other misfortune, and that we will respect the feelings and property of all, and on all occasions avoid giving offense by word or deed, and in any way acting contrary to the spirit and meaning of the foregoing By-Laws and Resolutions. For the faithful performance of all which we mutually pledge our lives, our fortunes and our sacred honor.

J.P. Van Hagen	J.B. Van Hagen	Thomas Rickey
Aaron Perrin	Samuel Connell	John M. Starr
William Donellan	William C. Abbey	Benjamin Stermann
J.P. Burns	James R. Torns	J.W. Ingraham
L.B. Sweet	W.S. Logsden	C.C. Lyman
D.M. Morrison	Joseph Thompson	Wash Anson
Asa Shinn	George Eggleston	William Cooke
William S. Cooke	John Yates	George Madeira
James Logan	R.G.F. Davis	C.S. Dorsey
C.M. Keeney	James Wolcott	Alva M. Emerson
F. Thompson	R. Evans	J. Railsback
M. Enego	Edward Wilson	S.P. Dorsey
A. Glasburn	A.H. Shafer	Taylor M. Sargent
Joshua B. Persoll	Isaac Stermann	J.H. Rickey
Milford B. Myers	D.R. Griffin	William L. Upchurch
Martin Schultes	George Shunk	Lines D. Cook

George Cook

William R. Marshal

Robert McNair

Cyrus McMyrtle

W. Jones

James Rickey

J.D. Carr

William Thompson

William McKay

Robert McMellon

William M. Byers

J. Styner

J.R. Cooke

J.D. Cross

Dan Madeira

J.W. Brown

Freeman Hathorn

Thomas McMellon

F.A. Madeira

A.S. Bemis

J.H. Colyer

Thomas W. Cooke

S.G. Baldwin

Richard Dorsey

We arrived at Elk Horn River about four o'clock; found lots of teams waiting for ferriage. We camped alongside of the river, making a circle of our wagons to insure greater security during the night. Mr. Rickey's company were camped near us. Here Pa overtook us, to our great satisfaction, and we spent a pleasant eve together, for this outdoor life seemed to charm us in its novelty.

Indians came around us in numbers, and begged all the time. Ma gave one old fellow some molasses in a tin cup, he telling her by his signs that he had three pappooses. Ma tried to make him understand to bring the cup back, but he failed to do so. Our camp was quite liberal in gifts to the Indians, wishing thereby to keep friendly with them.

Our camp consisted of thirty wagons We should have camped near Mr. Rickey's, but his company was large, which made it difficult to collect the cattle. Our folks therefore elected Mr. Perrin captain, and he appointed the watch for the night. But we met with no annoyance from Indians, they seeming friendly.

Tuesday, May 12th. We were detained until nearly noon by the ferry. The oxen had to be driven into the river and made to swim across, a man on horseback leading the way. It was a long time before they would attempt to cross. The men shouted, and whipped and kicked the poor frightened creatures before they seemed to understand what they were to do. Some floated down stream a distance; others would go straight across. It was an exciting scene to us all. However, the river was only sixteen rods wide, so the oxen were soon over, once they got started. The ferriage is $2 a wagon, the charge at the Missouri River being but $1. But we got across in our turn, and then were among the Pawnee Indians, those on the other side being Omahas.

Mr. Gilbert and company have gone ahead. We have not seen him since Sunday. Today we only traveled about two miles to a good camping ground, and there we halted in sight of Mr. Rickey's company, also a Mr. D'Orsay's company, so we are not lonely at all.

I went to washing as soon as things were fixed, for with a baby to care for there's always something to wash. Our men and boys amused themselves by marching in a procession headed by a drum and fife, and each one carrying a gun or whatever weapon could be found, and thus equipped they visited the other camps. Indians were around watching the movememts of the men, and seemed doubtful of the meaning. When the men returned to camp they made such a noise they scared all the horses off in a full gallop, so then they had to go after them and bring them back to our camp.

A little episode occurred here. It appeared three or four wagons, not of our company, had gone ahead and were being annoyed by the Indians, so a man was despatched on horseback to warn and obtain help. He had not gone far when, looking back, he saw someone in pursuit, and fearing it to be an Indian, jumped off his horse and took to his heels and hid in the tall grass, leaving his horse for Mr. Indian. The pursuer proved to be one of his own men, so he got well laughed at for his fright, and would have lost his horse had not an Indian caught it and brought it to camp. This caused much merriment to us all. Mr. Perrin made the man give the Indian a dollar for his honesty.

Wednesday, May 13th. Started about six o'clock this morning. There was a heavy dew, therefore my clothes were wetter this morning than when I went to bed. I had to bundle them up back in the wagon. About nine o'clock the sun came out and dispelled the dew, and then what a beautiful sight the three companies presented. There were about fifty or sixty wagons, with their white tops gleaming in the sunlight, slowly wending their way along the beautiful prarie. It was a picture long to be remembered, and all seemed happy and contented.

We traveled on till noon, and when we halted the Indians

came around begging for corn and money. A man came riding in haste, telling us that one of the wagons in a company ahead of us had been stopped by Indians, and trouble was feared. Our company at once came to a halt, but no one seemed to know the real cause. But the men took up their weapons and got ready for a fight—somewhere. Fortunately a chief of the Pawnees was on a pony near the head of our company. Mr. Perrin communicated to him through a squaw who spoke some English, and the chief galloped off to ascertain the trouble ahead.

Then the cry was given, "Corral," which means turn back and form a circle for protection. So we feared a fight. But no one knew, and thus we were in suspense. But in time the chief returned with a man who said the Indian had been caught who stopped the wagon, and a few sharp cuts were administered with a whip the chief carried. We paid a small tribute in provisions, tranquility was restored, and on we proceeded to Platte River, where we halted to water our cattle. The chief accompanied us to the river, and each wagon donated something to him, so we gained his good-will.

We drove about two miles farther, and camped near Rickey's and D'Orsay's companies. I hung my wet clothes out again on the wagon wheels, but rain came on, and we had a wet night. William is appointed captain of the watch, and has therefore to be out all night. No sign of Indians. Thursday, Friday, and Saturday passed off without anything of importance.

We have now traveled the whole distance from the Missouri River on beautiful plains, the roads being level as the floor. On Saturday evening a terrible storm came up. Some of the largest hailstones I ever saw fell, but as I slept in the wagon I met with no inconvenience. But those who occupied tents had several inches deep of water. The wind blew in hurricanes all Sunday, but we are all "right side up with care."

Monday, May 18th. Here we are waiting to cross the ferry at

"Loup Fork," and as the ferryman is going to Kanesville, I thought it good chance to send this by him. It is not written as I intended, but it's sent off in a hurry.

We met Mr. Gilbert here on Saturday, and he had been here three days. He left here for farther up stream to ford the river, but we prefer ferrying, as there is a risk to run in fording, so I am fearful we may not meet Mr. Gilbert again. This I shall regret very much, he being a good Christian man, and he always endeavors to have some religious service on Sunday.

Yesterday (Sunday) was very stormy and cold. We had one of the stoves moved into Ma's tent, cut a hole in the side and fixed a tin plate for the chimney to pass through. My dear little girl is quite well and brown as a berry. She has not commenced cutting teeth yet, but she says "Dad-Dad" so sweetly. I have knitted one baby sock, but could not do it your pattern, so a lady showed me another stitch easier. My side and ankle have got quite well, and when sissy is asleep I walk an hour or so. I wear bloomers, as do most of the women folks in the different companies. Ma, William, myself and the young ones bathed in a creek the other evening. I took baby along. She liked it so much. I wore my flannel gown for a bathing suit; so it was good we did not cover it as we intended.

How I wish I could some way get a letter from you. I do long to know how you all are. We are now thinking of going to California via Oregon, as we then escape a dreaded desert, and William thinks he would take up land in Oregon. A great many are so doing. The road that way is better, too.

We have not seen the Newby's yet. Did you get my letter and a paper from Kanesville? Pa wrote a letter to the Dubuque Herald, and he requested them to send you a copy, also to put you down as subscribers, Mr. Willis requesting him so to do.

Your nice horse nets William would not part with. He will need them, as they say flies are bad on the road at times. I hope you will get this letter, though Ma thinks it doubtful. But I shall write every chance I have. I can never pay postage, as we have no stamps, and it would be useless to give a stranger five cents. Give kindest regards to all inquiring friends, uncle, aunt and cousins. Ask them all to write, and direct to us at Sacramento.

Good by, dearest sister. Affectionately yours,

Monday, May 18, 1852.

LUCY COOKE.

Dear baby is nine months old today. I have just put her in short clothes.

LETTER NUMBER FIVE.

In wagon on the Plains of Nebraska, May, 1852.

DEAR MARIANNE: I WROTE A LETTER AND LEFT IT with the ferryman at Loup Fork, as he stated he was going to Kanesville, and would mail it and about a bushel more. Ma thought it doubtful if you ever received it. I have not written since then, but will now try and give some little account of our travel. We had to wait at Loup Fork from Saturday to Tuesday before a chance to cross, and then had to swim all the oxen. That was a tiresome job, as the river is wide at this point and full of quicksands. William earned a dollar by swimming a horse over for a man. I took the dollar for safe-keeping, but unfortunately I had a hole in my pocket, and so lost it. We drove about six miles that day, and then camped at such a beautiful place. It was just lovely. I went into the river to bathe in the evening, but no one would go in with me as such a cold wind was blowing, but I enjoyed it very much. For two or three days nothing unusual has occurred, so you lose but little by my not keeping a regular journal. We were very anxious to meet again with Mr. Gilbert's company, which had gone some distance up the Platte to ford.

On Thursday evening, May 21st, we had traveled twenty-eight miles from the ferry, and just as we were going to bed Mr. Perrin, our captain, found four of his horses and a mule were missing. William, with others, volunteered to go back in pursuit, thinking soon to overtake them. They rode about ten miles, saw nothing of them, and being in their shirt sleeves, returned to camp and prepared for a ride all night back to Loup Fork, as the men all thought that the point the horses had gone to. We saw nothing of them returning during the night, and I got awfully nervous about my husband. In the morning our train resumed its march. We loaned oxen to Mr. Perrin in place of horses. We here learned of Mr. Rickey's company being about eleven miles ahead, but he was alike unfortunate with ourselves, as eleven of his horses got away the same night. So now they were detained. We learned later that they found them all. William and the two men returned with our horses, having been abesent one day and two nights in their saddles. They found the horses standing at Loup Fork, waiting to cross. On their return some mean wretch cut off the ears of one of the horses in the night. Was it not shameful! They were a fine matched pair of carriage horses. Oh, but Mr. Perrin was angry.

On Friday, the 22d, we started early, but it was a wet morning and rained fast all day, and judge of our discomfort on arriving at our camping ground with everything wet to find no wood for fires. Oh, how miserable I did feel, with my baby needing a warm corner, and I felt how much I would have given could we step into your snug home and enjoy a warm supper. Our men cut up one of the horse feed boxes to make enough fire to fry some meat and boil some coffee, but all the clothes had to remain wet until the next day, when better luck was hoped for.

Saturday, May 23d. Today we passed a buffalo skull stuck in the ground, on which was the information that Rickey's company had passed there that morning. We passed three graves today of persons who died in '49 or '50. This evening we camped at a nice place, having plenty of grass, wood and water, so the wagons were emptied and things put out to dry and sun. There were three other camps in sight, so we had plenty of company. Here we stayed all Sunday. Some of us went to preaching in another camp about half a mile distant. We had a good bathe in a creek. The speaker was a plain Methodist. He took for his text, ''If ye then being evil know how to give good gifts unto your children,'' etc. I enjoyed the service. It seemed a treat, and a restful calm came o'er me through the day. In the evening a prayer-meeting was held in Pa's tent, and quite a good attendance. Thus was passed our third Sabbath on these vast plains.

Well, now I'll go back and give details of our last week's travel, though there was little variety, as it was all on level plain. One day we met three wagons returning, and on stopping to learn the cause, found the men at the heads of the two families had died suddenly. The widows were now returning to their friends. Poor women! They had our sympathy. Most of the past week Pa has amused himself hunting, but killed only birds till yesterday, when he shot and killed a buffalo. He carried some of the meat to the men's tent in the evening, which they all had for supper. I was not able to eat it, having a very sore mouth and throat. My tongue is so swollen and in such ulcers that I'm unable to talk much, and can swallow nothing but liquid food. I never had my tongue so sore before.

Sunday, May 31st. Today we have laid by, Pa having resolved not to travel on Sunday unless compelled, consequently the Perrins left us. So now we have none left of those who started with us. Our company is very busy (if it is Sunday) airing their clothing and things in the wagons. Many teams passed us while camping today, and one large flock of sheep went by, bound for Salt Lake City. This evening a prayer-meeting was held close by. Pa and Ma attended, but I was too poorly. A doctor passed us today to visit some cholera patients among the sheep herders. They are camped only a little distance off.

Monday, June 1st. Today we started early, and have passed over some awful sandy roads. It seemed almost impossible for the cattle to pull through. We have just met the doctor above mentioned, and learn from him that two of the men died last night, and another was dying this morning. The doctor said it was not much to be wondered at, as they had nothing with them to eat but bacon, hot bread and coffee. No rice, beans, pickles, or anything necessary on such a journey. We hear much talk of the cholera, but so far as we have seen, people frighten themselves into it; whilst some have improper food. Where there is such pure air I fail to see how it can be epidemic except for want of proper provisions.

This evening we camped alongside of a creek. We have only a small party with us now, for each company, when they have traveled a few weeks, fancy some plan of theirs is better than the rest, and thus agree to separate and go their way independently. Thus we lag behind, having stopped for Sunday.

Tuesday morning, June 2d. Today we started very early (four o'clock) so to lay by in the heat of the day. We traveled an hour before sunrise. I was quite cross at being awakened in the middle of the night, for so it seemed. But we stopped at 11 and started again at 2, and then traveled till 6, and camped by a creek and the Platte River. Ma, Lillie and I went and bathed, but it is a nasty, muddy stream, with a swift current. Still a bath seems always to benefit, and it's our only chance for ablution.

Close by our camp were some folks who had a sick woman with them. I went to see if we could help any. Found she had had cholera, but was getting better. We did what we could for her relief and then had to leave her.

Wednesday, June 3d. We again met with the sick woman. Pa and Ma went up and spoke with her. She seemed much better, and had quite a talk. She said her husband had just died of cholera. We soon passed them, though unwilling to leave the poor creature in the plight, but we could do nothing more. About an hour after a man rode past us and informed us that she was almost dead then, and that the men in whose company she was were stopping to dig her grave, before she was dead! There's humanity on the Plains! We could not believe the woman was dead. Think she was under the influence of laudanum, which the men were giving pretty freely.

This evening we came up to a landmark, a lone tree. Our guide book informs us we shall see no more trees for two hundred miles. We plucked a sprig or two for mementoes for friends, but as many already have done the same, only one branch is left. Tonight we camped by the side of a nice stream, but very shallow, and it being a very warm evening, Ma, myself and children went and paddled for nearly an hour. I undressed baby and let her sit in it, and oh, how she enjoyed it, and I to see her delight. Toward night a windstorm came up and blew down one of our tents; but that was nothing, we were getting used to such trifles.

Near by were five men who draw a truck. We first saw them last Sunday, and our boys made lots of fun of them, telling them there was lots of good grass for their cattle where we were, etc. The men seemed contented with their mode of travel and success. But we pitied them, and thought, How could they start on such a journey with such an outfit. All for the love of Gold.

We have had a long drive today, twenty-seven miles, so says our guide book, in order to reach camping ground. We are now in sight of Rickeys, and a short distance ahead of Perrins, so we have made as good time as those who traveled on Sunday. We passed the five men with their truck. Poor fellows. It had broken down, and they have now taken pieces of it for poles, and thus slung on their provisions, and carry on their shoulders. I pity them. I should like to know how far they get on their journey in this fashion. Surely they will soon give out.

We have had a very pleasant day for travel, the sun having been clouded, and rain fell last night. There are large numbers of teams on this great highway, and we hear thousands are behind us. Last week the mail carrier passed us on his way to Fort Laramie. We fear he will leave before we reach there to mail our letters. We met a company returning from California, they being the first met going in an opposite direction.

Oh, dear, the mosquitoes here are as thick as the sands, so for the first time we put on our horse nets. They were fine, though too small for our horses, coming but little lower than their sides. Our horses are very aristocratic, and the nets seem to make them feel more so.

We have all been over to Rickey's camp and had such a pleasant time. So now if possible we wish to keep near enough to spend our Sundays together.

Friday, June 5th. Started this morning as what to me seemed a ridiculous time, three o'clock. Ma and I and the young ones continued our sleep till about ten. Then we laid by for two or three hours by the side of a creek to let the cattle feed. We played a nice joke on Rickeys by starting so early, for they had taken the bells off their cattle so not to waken us with their early start. But we proved the smarter, as they knew nothing of our going till we passed their camp.

Saturday, June 6th. We stayed by the side of the Platte River today. Ma, Lillie and I went in bathing, which we do at every opportunity. So does dear baby; she enjoys it as much as we. This time we had a poor camping ground, with little or no grass. So on Sunday, the 7th (William's twenty-fifth birthday), we had to travel farther, and had no chance for Sunday services. My throat continues very bad. I used sugar of lead once, but the taste was so bad and turned my teeth so black I could not endure it again. I now keep sucking alum, which cleanses my mouth, but beyond that does very little good.

Wednesday, June 10th. Here we are opposite Fort Laramie, it being on the other side of the river. Oh, what a treat it does seem to see buildings again. My dear husband has just been over to the store there to see if he could get anything to benefit me, and bless him, he returned loaded with good things, for which he had to pay exorbitantly. He bought two bottles of lemon syrup at $1.25 each, a can of preserved quinces, chocolate, a box of seidlitz powders, a big packet of nice candy sticks, just the thing for me to keep in my mouth, and several other goodies. Oh, it all seemed a Godsend to me, and I was so careful of everything that I hated myself for my seeming selfishness in not dividing the candy with the children every time they looked anxiously at it. The preserved quinces seemed so grateful to my poor throat, and I took such tiny swallows of them each time, and then hung the can up overhead to the wagon bows. William bought a small bottle of ink also. It was only a ten-cent bottle, but he paid thirty cents for it. He says it's a splendid store over at the Fort, and it was crowded with people, and clerks were as busy as at any large city store. There are but few soldiers stationed here now, they being up on the Humboldt to protect the Governor who is appointed to Salt Lake. There are six or eight buildings at the Fort, and warehouses, bakeries, etc.

I am very weak from my sore tongue and throat, as my appetite is very poor. It seems wonderful that dear baby keeps well. She is the picture of health, and each day gets more and more engaging. William several times has taken her to bathe when I felt too poorly. I think probably we shall go via Oregon, as many think that way preferable. We then come to settlements five hundred miles sooner.

We have now passed over the two hundred miles without timber, and it seems good to see trees again. "Buffalo chips" have been our only fuel during these two hundred miles. I get very tired of this continuous riding, and wish often it were possible to step into your cozy home.

We are now in sight of Laramie Peak, but failed to see the buffaloes that are in that picture at Mrs. Telfair's in Davenport, but perhaps that Indian killed them. We have seen no Indians for two weeks now. These are the Sioux, and a noble-looking tribe they are; so well dressed: such gay trappings on them and their ponies, and beautiful beaded work they wear. We have had good success with our cattle so far, and only two or three have had sore feet. I hear we are going to have another calf soon. We have two cows for leaders to each wagon. One of our men killed an antelope the other day; they said it was delicious, tender eating. I have entirely lost my taste, so that anything dainty is lost on me. I just live on chocolate, for we have milk in plenty, and currant bread. We have a nice cook now. John R. gave up cooking some time ago, and it goes much better without him. He now takes his turn in driving the oxen.

My baby cries so I cannot fill this sheet as I desired. I shall most likely write again from Fort Hall or Salt Lake. The latter we don't pass if we go to Oregon. But if we should go to Salt Lake we expect to spend the Fourth of July there. I intend to continue writing often as I can, but my throat is so bad I cannot write regularly. William send love to yourself and husband, and best remembrances to all inquiring friends. We have not seen Mr. Gilbert's company again. I hope you are writing long letters to me, to Sacramento City. Good bye.

Lovingly, your affectionate sister,

LUCY COOKE.

LETTER NUMBER SIX.

Nebraska Territory, June 10, 1852.

EAREST SISTER: I MAILED MY LAST TO YOU FROM Fort Laramie yesterday, and now commence another epistle. The road from the Fort changes considerably. We have now passed over "The Plains," and glad I am, for there was so little to interest on them.

Yesterday, the 9th, we traveled about eighteen miles and camped near Rickey's and several other companies on the banks of the Platte. Oh, what rough riding it was all day. But still the magnificent scenery made up for all inconvenience. We were long finding suitable camping ground, but the grass is here abundant on the hillsides, and very rich, so the men say.

June 11th. Have today come about twenty miles over plenty of rocks and stones. I have ridden the three days in one of the ox wagons, as I could better lie down there than in our own little crowded wagon, and I have been so poorly. My dear William waits on me hand and foot. What should I do without him? Bless him! My tongue improves but slowly, the ulcers seeming as large and thick as ever.

We are now entering the Rocky Mountains, so suppose shall have nothing but jolt, jolt. The mountains have such grand pines on them. You would enjoy the scenery. We are annoyed with a plant called the prickly pear or cactus. In some places it nearly covers the ground. There's plenty of wild sage around.

We are now traveling without a "guide," as the writer of the one we have used so far followed up the south side of the Platte from Fort Laramie, and we intend keeping on the north side, as it is said the grass is more abundant all the way. So that's good news.

Saturday, June 12th. Have had a very pleasant day's travel. Magnificent scenery! Very hilly. We met some "packers" today, which is always interesting, as each exchange traveling notes. We are still in sight of Laramie Peak, and have been the past five days. Tonight we are camped near the Platte, having traveled eighteen miles.

Sunday. Quite a cold morning. My dear husband had a bad toothache yesterday, and today his face is hideously swollen and he feels miserably. So now it's my turn to be nurse. I let him have his breakfast in bed, and made him some cornstarch porridge. We have had quite a busy day in airing things in the wagons, for Sunday is the only chance we get for such; work. The men mostly do their washing that day. We have just had supper, consisting of fish, rice, tomatoes and ham, with hot bread and tea.

I drink chocolate since I have been sick; I enjoy it better. I am thankful to say my mouth is better. I am using a gargle now, of sage tea, with borax, alum and sugar, and it is a great benefit. I wonder it never occurred to use it before, as the wild sage is abundant.

We have all been bathing today. "Sissy" enjoys it so much, and seems ready for a dash whenever we see water. How I have thought of you today, and your dear husband, jogging along side by side to Davenport to church, and the thought came: Shall I ever travel that road again with you? I don't know how I should feel were I to know it would never happen again, and I should not return to Iowa. Your home is now "the dearest spot on earth" to me. I must soon begin a letter to Uncle's folks at LeClaire. You will think my subjects very disconnected, but I have so often to quit writing and attend to other things. We found a sack of graham crackers today spoiled from damp, so they had to be thrown away, which in our situation is a loss. How is Caroline getting along, and how do the currant bushes look? Every tree and spot around your home is vivid in remembrance as though visited yesterday. How I should enjoy running over to Mrs. Wright's to supper, and see her lovely clean home. I told you in my last of the "Lone Tree," and promised a sprig therefrom. Will try to remember this time. Divide it with Sarah Wright and Margaret Coleman. Tell them it's the only tree we pass for two hundred miles.

Monday, 14th. Today we passed grand mountains, and for a considerable distance traveled in what seemed a river bed, as all the lines and traces of water were visible on the rocks. We camped about sundown but had poor grass.

Tuesday. We started this morning about four o'clock. Rode about six miles, then turned the cattle loose, there being rich grass. Stayed about an hour and a-half. Here Rickey's company all passed. But as we did not stop at noon, we passed them resting. Saw a dead mule in the road. Have traveled along where there were immense round rocks, like cannon balls. Surely this was from action of raging waters in the long-ago ages. The scenery here is wild and beautiful. Again we camped on the Platte. Have traveled about twenty miles today. Pa bought a cow of a man the other day; she had just calved. She seems an excellent animal. The price asked was only $20, so we are pleased, as we now have five cows. But there's such a bother to get the men to milk, and two are dry, that I frequently have to beg milk of others.

Wednesday. Today we have been traveling through deep sandy roads. Oh, how tedious it was. And tonight we are on poor camping grounds, and the only wood we have for camp is two wagon wheels the men picked up. There's a ferry near by on the Platte, which will be the last. The charges for crossing are enormous, $5 for each wagon, and then extra for men, horses and cattle. We, however, have no desire to go on the south side of the river.

Thursday. Today we have traveled twenty-six miles without any water, except what we hauled. Each member of the company carries a canteen with sufficient water to quench his thirst; but it gets pretty warm during the day. The water we passed today is strong alkali, in lakes. The poor oxen seemed to suffer for water, as the roads were very sandy and heavy pulling. The day has been quite warm, too. One lake we passed had a white substance (they say it's saleratus) all around the banks, six or eight inches in thickness. We picked some up for curiosity sake. When we had driven four or five miles we passed a dead cow. She was in a drove just ahead of us, and had drank of the alkali water. Tonight we have camped by a spring; but it's so small, and such crowds around (it being the only pure water for twenty-six miles) that it takes a long time to catch a bucketful. But it's our only chance for some distance.

We have now joined camp with a company from Dubuque, Iowa. They are all men. The gent who takes them through was constable there. We joined them because we soon shall be among the Crow Indians, and it's safest to be in large companies.

Friday. Have tonight arrived on the "Sweetwater," in which I bathed my baby. It has a very rapid current, so we did not care to test it ourselves. We are now in sight of "Independence Rock" and the Rocky Mountains. We expect to drive but little tomorrow, so to recruit the cattle. But the grass is poor tonight, and no wood.

Saturday. We have had a fine wild goose chase today after each other. In the morning we drove our horse wagon to "Independence Rock" and stayed there two or three hours examining names which are inscribed in every available place. Lillie and some others climbed to the summit, but as baby was awake I had to remain below. Most of our party added their names to those already there. (Shall I repeat what we sometimes have heard, "Fools' names, like their faces, are always seen in public places?") My dear William, however, refrained, saying it looked too much like hard work to climb the rough rock barefooted for the sake of passing his name to the future. Some names were cut in the rock, others done with tar, or white, black or red lead, and some few with paint. I could not recognize any as acquaintances, though some were familiar, and from our section in Iowa.

Our ox teams had gone on ahead, and with the intention of only driving to good grass, and then lay by till Monday. We followed along in our light wagon about two hours after, expecting of course to overtake them. We drove about four miles, and then came in sight of our folks. But at this point was another natural curiosity, vix., the "Devil's Gate." So we left our wagon to continue traveling, whilst Ma, Lillie, William and I and two or three of our young men walked up to the rock. It is a grand sight! Surely worth the whole distance of travel. The "Sweetwater" rushes through an opening in the rocks, the walls on each side rising several hundred feet perpendicularly, and as though riven in two by some great convulsion of nature. On one side projections, on the other side corresponding hollows, showing conclusively that in former ages no opening was there. Oh, it was a most wonderful and sublime sight. I wish 'twere in my power to describe it, but I cannot. I bathed dear little Sarah's feet in the rushing waters, and only wish she had been able to realize the grand occasion, which may never in her life be repeated.

I will now tell of our "chase." When we left the "Devil's Gate" it was about noon. We had to walk a distance before we overtook our wagon, which was awaiting us. Many tents were pitched on the banks of the Sweetwater, and we expected our company to be there. But not seeing them, we enquired at different camps, and each told us our folks had gone past between eleven and twelve o'clock, so were ahead. We therefore drove on and on, looking eagerly this side and the other. Meantime our appetites admonished us that it was a long time since breakfast, and seldom did we carry food in our wagon, and this was the first time we had wandered away from our food supply. Well, on and on we rode, till we felt pretty certain our folks must have turned off from the road, and consequently were behind us. But each company we passed said, "No, they were ahead." We were surprised at our company going so far, as it had been settled only to go six or eight miles and then wait for us, and I had quite a big washing to do when we struck camp. Well we drove about ten miles in all, and saw no signs of them. Had nothing to eat, and it was now near five o'clock. So we made our case known to and accepted the offer of a company called the "Bull Heads" (which sign was painted on their canvas wagon covers) to camp with them that night, though it seemed a strange experience to be lost on such a journey. But so it was.

We had occasionally met with this company, and William was slightly acquainted with one or two of them. Well you may be sure we were glad of our suppers, and they freely gave us of their fare. I ate biscuit, rice, stewed apples, and tea, then felt refreshed and better. The young men seemed a fine set of fellows, and enjoying their trip. One of our young men concluded to make further effort to find our company, so he continued walking, and at length reached Perrin's company, and on entering camp found Pa there and our cook, eating supper, but most dead with fatigue. All were astonished at thus meeting. It appears Pa and the cook had visited the "Devil's Gate" early in the morning, and then they followed along the road, and each time they enquired for our company were told, as we had been, that they were ahead. But the joke of it was, they had come across some good wood, and seeing but a poor chance for any along the road, they gathered enough to last over Sunday, and packed it between them past all camps, expecting each camp would be ours. They carried the wood four or five miles, then threw it away.

Then they met a man who said our tents were two miles back, so back they trudged; but at length they stumbled on Perrin's camp, which we had not seen for two or three weeks, and here it was our young man met with them, and then it was found in distance only about a mile from us to the "Bull Head" company. So after supper Pa walked over to fetch Ma, Lill and Richard to share Mrs. Perrin's hospitality. But William, myself and the two young men remained till next morning with our new friends, who at night amused themselves with dancing, in which William joined as heartily as any. Their cook on the previous day had found a bundle of woman's clothing, which he put on and had worn it all day, sun-bonnet and all, which had caused considerable merriment all along the road. So when dancing came off at night there was a great demand for this lady partner. So William came to where I was gone to bed (on the ground, by the way) and took my saque, dress and sun-bonnet to wear. What guys the two did look. But they all seemed to enjoy it, and I was amused till after dark looking at them.

Sunday. We ate our breakfast, thanked our friends for their hospitality, and then drove to our own folks, who remained on Perrin's camping ground, they having gone on ahead. Ma, William, Lill and I have been bathing in the "Sweetwater." The "Bull Heads" have camped close by and kept us in food till our teams arrived, which was not till about one o'clock, and then they made merry at our expense. But no matter, it made a nice little change, and no one hurt.

Thursday night. I have not noted our progress since Sunday. It has been so cold each evening that we have been only too glad to snug into our bed to keep warm. All Sunday and Wednesday we rode alongside the Rocky Mountains. They are indeed well named, for they are a mass of solid rocks. The roads have been awfully sandy, and alkali water abounds. On Wednesday we counted 26 head of dead cattle in consequence. We are so far fortunate in not losing any, but our drivers have to watch with vigilance and keep the cattle from drinking as we pass along. Today we have passed several banks of snow, so you may judge we are in high altitude. The mountains are white, and at night we camped alongside snow banks. We are near the Sweetwater on such a pretty spot; such lots of gooseberries growing.

We have a man in our camp taken very sick with cholera. He is not expected to live till morning. He has a family with him. Ma and I have just been to bathe in the Sweetwater, but oh, it was cold! We could only take two or three dips and then run out. What a strange country we are in. Here we are bathing alongside snow banks and in sight of mountains covered with it, whilst at same time grass is green and gooseberries growing in abundance. I picked some to stew, but they were pretty small.

Friday morning. The sick man is still alive, but very bad; has severe cramps. William has gone off to hunt a doctor in one of the camps. Has just found one who has tried to relieve the sufferer, and thinks he may recover. We shall remain here in camp all day on his account, for as they travel with us we could not well leave him behind. William and I amuse ourselves picking gooseberries. What a task it was. We gathered about a pint. I made two pies of them, and gave one to Ma. I had to roll my piecrust on the wagon seat;

rather primitive style, you'll think, but it seemed good to do even that bit of cooking. I just long to be housekeeping again.

Saturday morning. The sick man is a trifle better; some hopes of his recovery. We have only traveled about eleven miles today, on his account. This morning we arrived at the South Pass, after which all the water we see will be running to the Pacific.

Sunday. Today we drove a short distance to better camping ground, but the grass is not good. We are now camped near Rickey's. Ma, Pa, and some others attended service in their camp. Baby prevented my going. This afternoon William and I sang out of your hymn book; it brought several around who joined in, and we had quite a pleasant sing . . . . Since writing the above I upset my ink and lost my pen, consequently my writing has had to be abandoned for a while. But we have journeyed on and on each day, till we reached Fort Bridger, 113 miles from Salt Lake City. At this place Pa traded off some flour and an ox for a pretty Indian pony. The ox had been lame some time: his hoof was coming off. Pa gave seven bags of flour at $6 per hundred. Pa was offered $60 for the pony soon after, but he concluded to ride him on ahead to Salt Lake City and thus find good camping ground; also to see if any employment could be found for any of our men folks whilst we stayed in the city. William had decided to remain there till following spring, as we were so tired of being in the crowd, and had only come half our journey, but everything was so uncomfortable, and my health was poor the greater part of the journey, and I needed rest.

We reached the city July 8th, three days after Pa left us. I was very pleased with the appearance of the city. It seemed such a treat to see houses again, and to hear the chickens crowing as we entered the streets. I was so pleasantly taken with the change from our daily wanderings, that I hoped things might turn for us to remain a season there. Pa had met a man who owns a mill, and had spoken of William to him. The man promised to employ him and his team for the winter to haul timber from the mountains at $5 per day. William thinks he will do this as soon as the cattle recruit.

The day we arrived, July 8th, we camped opposite a boarding house, and Pa, wishing to give us a treat, ordered dinner for our family, and oh, when we sat down to the table I thought never did victuals look more tempting! We had roast beef, chicken, green peas, potatoes, pie, cheese, bread and butter and tea. I thought the bread and butter seemed the greatest treat; and then it all looked so clean, and the house was so trim and neat. But you will laugh when I tell that so unused were we to chairs that on entering the parlor we each and all dropped down on the floor and thus sat until one of us remarked the situation, when we all laughed, and forthwith arose and took chairs. But it seemed so funny. I quite hated to go back to our wagons after being in such a nice house.

We gained information of a Mr. Roberts (a Mormon), who was near neighbor of Pa's in Iowa City, but had come to this place to live. So the day after our arrival we started out to find his whereabouts, and succeeded in tracing him up without much trouble. He was living about eight miles out from the city, and was very glad to meet our folks, and wanted the whole family to come out to his place and stay while we remained in camp there. However, we did not accept this kind offer, but William and I and baby stayed with them all night to discuss the plan of our passing the coming winter in that valley.

Pa having passengers with him bound for Sacramento, it was deemed advisable for him to see them to their destination, and after much consultation it was arranged for him to proceed and leave Ma and the family here for the winter, and in the event of Pa's safe arrival in California he could decide on a location and send for Ma and the family in the spring. John, Richard and Thomas are left to care for them during the winter. John has the two horses and wagon, to do teaming for their support.

Ma has rented a little house in town, and William and I are still with Mr. Roberts, and I assure you we hear Mormonism from morn till night. The doctrine seems a queer affair, and the men seem to believe in Polygamy to a great extent, and are taking wives after the "sealing" process. It seems disgusting to us, but we have to keep quiet over it, for emigrants seem to be watched by the people here.

One day I was out riding with Sissy in an ox wagon with Mr. Roberts, and he was trying to impress me with his religion, and soon he talked of the sealing of women to Mormon husbands, and thus their safety was insured in the next world. A Mormon was privileged to have many women "sealed" to him. But if they remained with "Gentile" husbands their future was doomed. The man kept on in this "convincing" strain as we jogged along the country road, and finally he magnanimously offered to take me, baby and all, and have me "sealed" to him and thus have my entrance secured in the Celestial City, providing I would leave William and cling to this old scamp's skirts.

You can imagine how this proposition was received by me! The old scamp! With his slipshod gait and lank figure; with his long, unkempt hair, almost down to his shoulders—a rare prize, he! How William did laugh when I got home and told him the offer I had from Sydney Roberts.

We remained with the old Mormon for two or three weeks deciding what employment would be for William, and arranged to go out to a shingle mill to haul logs for it, and we can occupy a cabin there. William is to be paid in shingles, which are good as the cash, and can find ready sale in the city. John is to join William in the hauling. We have a wagon and two yoke of cattle for their use, and $6 or $7 a day they can earn, so that's what William expects to be engaged in during the winter here.

I really have so much I'd like to tell I don't know what first to relate. I suppose you know this Salt Lake Valley is entirely occupied by Mormons, or "Latter Day Saints." We have heard them so often spoken of with contempt, but so far as we have seen they are very hospitable and kind to us "Gentiles," though we understand matters enough to be guarded in our speech respecting them or their doctrines, for there seems a strict surveillance kept over all outsiders. But we get along first rate so far, and it's a treat for us to be alone in our own little cabin, instead of the slow-going travel, with not over-congenial associates, which has been our lot now for two months. I was very sick of it all.

Our little cabin at the shingle mill has an open fireplace on one side, and as there's plenty of shingle blocks for fuel at the mill close by, we at night have a cheery blaze to sit by, and thus don't miss the candles, for no tallow is to be had for illuminating purpose. There are two bunks by the wall opposite the fire. William sleeps in the upper and baby and I in the lower, which makes us comfortable, and I enjoy doing the little bit of cooking.

Last Saturday (24th of July) was a great day with the Mormons, it being the fourth anniversary of their arrival in the valley. There was to be a big procession and grand jubilee. We went into town to see it all and stay at Ma's. The Mormons marched around their Tabernacle block headed by brass bands of stirring music, and everybody seemed merry and happy. (It seemed so strange out in the wilderness.) Foremost in the procession were twenty-four old ladies (their board of health). These were dressed in black, with squares across their shoulders. They looked so neat and nice. The foremost two carried a banner inscribed "Mothers in Israel!" "Our Children are Our Glory." Then a number of old men, who were the bishops. I could not see what was on their flag. Then came twenty-four young ladies in white dresses and blue silk scarfs tied over one shoulder and under the arm, straw hats and blue ribbons. Their banner was inscribed "The Virtue of Utah." Then came twenty-four little girls in white frocks, with blue spencers, straw hats and wreaths of roses. Next came little boys in white trousers and buff jackets, straw hats and ribbons, and lastly a big procession of men, each one carrying some instrument or implement used in his trade. It was a very pretty sight. They all marched into the Tabernacle, which is a grand big building, with seating capacity for 2500. There are four large doors, one at each corner, which admit a good breeze and ready exit. There are no galleries, but the seats all rise from the front, where the speakers are. It seemed wonderful to find such a concourse of people here.

I have attended service here once on a Sunday. The singing was so nice, led by an Englishman who sings familiar English tunes. The building is always full at every service. I did not care for the harangue of the speakers, but the novelty of the scene interested me.

The city contains a goodly number of English proselytes, but a chief beauty is the little trenches on each side of every street, through which runs a clear, pretty stream, cold from the adjacent mountains. This abundant irrigation produces wonders of vegetation, and vegetables are a delight. We are getting somewhat acquainted, and frequently attend picnics. Then the watermelons are a sight to behold.

I told you Pa bought an Indian pony at Fort Bridger. Well, on the fourth day after our arrival here it was found dead in the field. Pa stayed ten days in the city, and then continued his journey to California with his passengers.

Whilst we were visiting at Ma's, in came "John Richards," bringing Clarence Whiting and one of the Newby boys. We were delighted to see them, and I soon found they had letters for me. I felt certain of a lengthy one from you, dear sister, but oh, not a line. But there were several notes from English friends, which dear

Uncle had brought from England. One from Mrs. Scott and one from dear Mrs. Shepperson and little Jane Critchley. But each concluded not to write much, expecting Uncle John would meet me and "tell it all," Mrs. Shepperson sent me a pretty neck piece and Jane said her sister had given Uncle some pretty pieces for dresses for the baby, which I suppose you have got. I think Uncle might have written me somewhat of his English visit, don't you?

William has been working in the harvest field, his wages being $2 per day. We are entirely destitute of everything for housekeeping, and such things are sold very high. Groceries are enormous. Sugar, 3 pounds for $1; coffee and tea, $2; dried apples, 40 cents; soap, 20 cents per bar. So we don't do much washing, and there's not grease enough to make soft soap. Wood is $10 per cord, it having to be hauled eight or ten miles from the canyons. Dry goods are very high too, very common calico being 25 or 30 cents a yard; ribbons, the cheapest, $1 a yard.

I am glad I did not cover my flannel dressing gown with that dress pattern, as it will be more useful made up itself. I have no bonnet but my old sun-bonnet, and I use the parasol you gave me. I think living here will teach us economy, and that's worth learning. William says if he can make a good living here he may remain, and not go to California, but return to Iowa in four or five years. This valley is a lovely fertile spot. We are about eight miles distant from the mountains on one side, and about twenty distant from them on the other side. When it rains it's interesting to see the clouds resting on the mountains about half way down. We are twenty miles distant from the Great Salt Lake, the waters of which are so salt that from three barrels of water one of salt is obtained, and it's beautiful, and clear as crystal.

Clarence Whiting is going to remain here awhile, and perhaps will work at the mill William is to be employed at. The Newby Brothers have gone on to California in good spirits. William traded a yoke of his cattle for a yoke of ours, his being footsore from travel, whilst ours, from two weeks' rest, had recovered. Oh, what fine feed is here for stock; cattle keep fat all winter, and with no more care than in summer, so they tell us. William Newby tells us Mr. Willis is talking of selling out and going to California in the spring. But I guess it's only talk. Well, so far as we have come, there's nothing to fear on the road. Two-thirds of the distance has been good as a turnpike road. We had two mountains to descend, the Wasatch, some few miles back from here, which were very steep and long, and at one place our wagons were let down by ropes. But it sounds worse than it really was, for we had no breakdowns at any bad place. We heard great talk of things being thrown away on the road, but we saw little that was of any good cast away, excepting stoves, and of these there were plenty. I wonder people took such things, as an iron bakeoven, with frying pan and iron pot to cook out of doors, is far preferable to a stove.

The folks where we are staying drink wheat coffee, and to me it seems a very nourishing drink; but of course you have to get accustomed to it. Potatoes are very fine. People are cultivating the sugar beet, and machinery is now on the way from France to manufacture it into sugar. Molasses is now being made. They say it's a very simple process; I may try some. There's but little fruit here yet. Bushes on mountain sides produce a small berry called the "service berry," or "sarvis," as they have it, and parties go out in its season to gather them. Our neighbors are going today. I am going to keep house. They take a tent and stay all night, as they go quite a distance. The berries are very sweet when ripe, requiring no sugar. They are also dried for winter.

Those horse nets you made us we have let Mr. Roberts have. He is to make us a table for them. Pa bought Ma a table and had to pay $10 cash for it, and it's a very common kitchen table at that. William has ordered three chairs and a bedstead for us. It will be no fancy one, either. Sheets we have none. But no matter, for "sleep to the laboring man is sweet." That will, I trust, include his wife and baby. I happen to have brought a few towels, tablecloths and pillow slips with us, and had we known of stopping here this winter there's many little things I might have brought.

There's a lovely creek close by here, surrounded by bushes, and every day I take Sissy down there to bathe and paddle around on its pebbly shore; she loves it so much. She has not yet cut a single tooth, and nearly a year old! She is not yet weaned, and it's doubtful when she will be. I dread it so much. She won't stay five minutes away from me, and I have to carry her everywhere I go, and she's so fat and heavy I get so tired sometimes. I fear she may be taking whooping cough, as it's around, and she begins to cough. She still sucks those two fingers.

We are yet sleeping in our wagon. I much prefer it to the house. William has taken the wagon bed off the running gear, and it stands on the ground across the road from the house, so that is our home for the present. We still have a tent, which we shall use when we go to the mill. All the people seem to use their wagon beds to keep their things in outside their house, for of course the covers are on tight. The houses are all made of unburned bricks called adobes, or "dobies," and the buildings look very neat and pretty.

Emigrants are arriving every day, and some of the Mormons drive quite a brisk business by going out fifty or sixty miles on the road to sell their garden stuff, butter, chickens and eggs to the incoming emigrants, for after a two-months' journey in ox wagons such things meet with ready sale. Then another good chance for money-making is with the sore-footed cattle, as emigrants will trade off two yokes for one in good condition. In a few weeks, with rest and good feed, the weary ones recruit and can readily be traded again, one for two. The cows here are a sight. They get so large. I never saw any elsewhere so fine and sleek. Pigs seem quite scarce; I have only seen two or three as yet. William wishes he had brought a grain drill through, it would be a fortune to possess.

My writing is poor, and the subjects so disconnected. But Sissy stands jigging by my side and takes my attention. How I wish you could see her; she looks so sweet, I think. She wore the pretty red saque you made her, the other day, and it was much admired. Snow is on the distant mountains, although here it is so hot.

John Richards came from town today to see us. He says Ma has sold the cow Pa left with her to a cabinet maker, who is to let her have a bedstead and six chairs. That will seem quite citified.

I find the mail goes out in a day or two, so as I have about told everything, I may not write again till I hear from you. I hope then to hear all the news. Give lots of love to Uncle's family, and do try and get them all to write. I wonder if Cousin Lydia is married yet to Edward Russell. I wish Emma was here to take baby and wean her. If Ma was like most grandmas, she'd take her, but it's useless to look to her. Well, I must conclude, for this is a long letter, and maybe will tire you all. William joins in love to you both, also Uncle.

Ever your affectionate sister,

LUCY COOKE

Write to me at Great Salt Lake City, Utah Territory.
Last of July, 1852.

LETTER NUMBER SEVEN.

Salt Lake, October, 1852.

EAREST SISTER: JUST TO WHILE AWAY A SUNDAY afternoon, I sit me down to write again, though I quite expect a letter from you when the mail arrives. How often are you the subject of our conversation. I wish I were seated in your snug parlor, telling the wonders of travel. But writing must suffice. I hope you received my last, written soon after our arrival, so I will try to take up my narrative near where I left off.

William assisted Mr. Roberts with his harvesting, after which he cut hay for our two yoke of oxen, for as they are to be worked through the winter, of course feed has to be provided. We lived in Mr. Roberts' family four or five weeks, and then we pitched our tent opposite their house, so I did my own cooking, which we best enjoy. I like living in a tent in fine weather, but oh, when the windstorms come, then it's terrible! Ours is a good tent, but the dust cannot be kept out. We lived thus about six weeks and then moved to the mill which I before spoke of, in a snug little cabin one roomed, close by the mill and two houses, one occupied by Alexander, the mill owner, and the other by his brother and family. So we don't lack company; but all are Mormons.

The furniture of the cabin consists of four shingle blocks for seats and a rickety wash bench for company, and our table is quite a primitive affair. The chairs and bedsteads mentioned in a former letter we did not get. There's a mantle-piece over the fireplace, and for ornaments on it I have that tin water bottle like yours, a tin "feeder," a box of mustard (for sickness), William's bowie knife, his razor strop and silver-keyed flute. A rare set of ornaments, surely, you'll say. I often look at them and compare with your pretty mantel. Ah, me, what a difference! But it's all good enough for our present need, and so we are contented and happy together generally. We have our wagon cover overhead for a ceiling. We have no crockery at all, all tinware and but little of that. We find many difficulties to contend with, as William has only commenced earning, so we had to do without everything but common necessities.

We had only one dollar's worth of sugar (2½ pounds), which we made last four or five weeks. I happened to have a bit of Castile soap in my little box and that had to do two washings. I don't claim to be any washer so as long as I can find in my box anything to give away in payment, I got a young girl to come in and do it. But my treasures were soon exhausted; then I had to do it, ah me! Our food consisted principally of flour and potatoes, and sometimes we did not sit to our table in a very thankful mood. William got a small piece of bacon once or twice, and we stood over it marking it off in sections for each day, to see how long it would last. And sometimes he stood over me and begged just one little piece more, for it was good.

One day Mrs. Alexander had been baking bread, and she kindly brought me a great thick slice of warm bread with squash! I ate it as a rare dainty. I got better acquainted with a woman some distance off who kept a cow and had a little butter to sell. This I managed to get by trading off my few baby clothes, as she was soon to need them.

If William gets to work steady we soon shall be able to live in more comfort; but the work is very hard. He had injured his back several times lifting logs, so he had to lay by. He uses but one yoke of oxen, and has rented the other to a man who works with him. Before the days were so short he could chop and haul a load a day, which would make 2000 shingles, and his pay was half for hauling. They are worth $10 per thousand, which is considered good pay. William only reckons to work half his time, as it would be too hard on oxen or man. The canyon they haul from is about two miles from here, but they go five miles up it to the timber, and the roads are fearful; nothing but rocks. Every day wagons break down on the trip. William has traded off his wagon for a tremendous heavy one, so he has only broken the reach twice and turned over once!

The snow begins to cover the mountains. Winter is near. We expect next week to do a little trading in town and lay in for winter much as we can, for groceries will soon be bought up, long before more can arrive across the plains. We already have a nice lot of potatoes, squash and sugar beets, These latter are not grown in the states. The seed comes from France; from which sugar is made. They are delicious eating. We have now plenty of meat, as William bought a hind quarter of beef, and so we live more comfortably, but I still do miss the groceries.

Dear William tries to cheer me by telling he'll soon get all I need. Any way, we have fared better than Ma has in the city, for John does but poorly at providing for a family, though I don't think he's lazy. But they manage so poorly, so that when we go there to see them there's nothing but bread and potatoes. Fortunately, whenever they have been out to see us we have had a bit of butter for our bread, or something different to their fare. Sometimes I make a pudding and put in some ''sarvice berries;''

that goes good. I often think of all your preserves, and the sugar to be had at ten or twelve pounds for a dollar.

Dear Sister: Since writing the above, your letter dated, September 13th has been received. Oh, how delighted I was to hear from you! My letter was the first received since we left the States. Ma was very anxious to know if any of her friends were mentioned in it. But you said nothing of them. You don't seem to have a very high opinion of this people. Neither have I; and much will you be astonished (but perhaps not) when I tell you that about five weeks ago I witnessed the baptism of Ma, she having joined the Mormon Church. It took place on Sunday morning. We all drove out in a wagon to a suitable spot on the "Jordan," and there the Mormon elder who accompanied us performed the ceremony in the stream. William would not go with us, so he stayed home and took care of baby. He made some very uncomplimentary remarks about the Mormons and their doctrines, and was annoyed to think Ma had decided to join them. Next Sunday John and Lill are to be baptized! My only fear is Ma may influence my dear William. No fear about myself, and not much at present regarding him.

I'm so glad we live out from the city and its influence, as we cannot often be expected to attend their meetings. Ma says we lose much from not having this privilege. But I am willing, and don't count it a loss. It annoys me to write of the Mormons, and still more to know any of the family have joined them. But I think Ma always was a fanatic on religion. She says she has fasted and prayed to be shown the Truth, and feels now she has found it.

I will now refer to your letter. And so the horse "Old Bones" is dead. William laughed at that. But you will miss the faithful, though homely, animal. Well Cousin Lydia is married. I thought that would happen soon. This letter, as you may suppose, is taken up and laid down so many times. After each line or two sometimes a week or more intervenes, and since the last was written we have heard from Pa in California. Ma received thirteen letters in the last mail. I now feel so full of news I can settle to nothing, but want to talk it all to William. Pa seemed to have had a good time getting through with his passengers. and I don't think he lost any cattle, though some nearly gave out when crossing the desert. Two oxen laid down and moaned from exhaustion, and after a while there was a chance to buy some water of men who had come out a way on the desert for the purpose of selling it. Pa paid 75 cents a bucketful, which saved the cattle. He afterwards passed a place where it was for sale at $5 per bucket. One cow gave out, and they would have had to leave her, but Pa met a "relief train" from California, which bought her. Gave Pa $50 and a good breakfast for all his men and feed for the cattle. The balance of the cows fetched $100 each. The oxen only brought $100 per yoke, they being in poor condition.

Pa visited many of the principal cities or mining towns. I tell you all this from memory, as of course Ma has his letters in town. Times were then very dull, it being the dry season, and when his first was written he had not obtained any business position. But in his last letter he was engaged to superintend a farm a short distance from San Francisco. Its owners live in the city. There are five hired men on it. Pa has a nice house to live in, a housekeeper also, and a horse to ride. He says he bathes in the Pacific every morn. His salary is $75 the first month, just what he asked. He has no labor to do himself, only superintend. We wonder how he manages, as he is no farmer. But he says he engaged with the firm on William's account, thinking we should be glad of a place to go on in the spring when we arrived there. Pa had not received Ma's letter telling of her joining the Mormons, so he don't know he has to return here, for Ma now will remain. Pa is always good to leave Ma to judge of religious matters, and so what she believes is right he will follow. How nice to have such trust in each other. But he said before he left he was almost a Mormon, so I guess he had given the matter some thought.

He speaks very highly of California and its products. Says he intends purchasing lands for his boys, William included (pity he did not), as so far as his observation has gone, farming seems the most profitable way of making a living. He wrote me a very kind letter. Said he did it to tell me he loved me.

Mr. and Mrs. William Hubbard, the latter with whom I boarded in Moline soon after our marriage, were in company with Mr. Gilbert, whom I have before mentioned, and he was to take them through to California. But they got dissatisfied, as almost every one seems to on this trip. We have had our annoyances, which is putting it mildly, and we desired to leave our company. But Pa was so unwilling, therefore we decided to remain here all winter, and make a fresh start in the spring with a fresh company. Mr. and Mrs. Hubbard have also decided to remain, and so we may go together.

In the former part of this letter I told you we expected to go to town to make our first purchases for housekeeping, of course only the most primitive scale. Well, we have been, and I'll tell you what we invested in. William got $8 a thousand cash for his shingles. So we bought a small bread pan, $1.50; a small camp kettle with lid, $2, tin coffee pot, $1, and a little tin bucket with lid, $1. So there was $5.50 in as many minutes. But I assure you, had they all been silver, I could not have felt greater pride in their possession. Then we went to a provision store and made the following purchases: Twelve pounds of sugar at 40 cents; 5 pounds of coffee at 40 cents; half pound of tea at $2 a pound; half gallon molasses at $3 per gallon; 1 pound saleratus, 40 cents; 2 bars soap at 50 cents; a pretty woolen dress for me at 50 cents; and lastly a pair of buckskin mittens for William, $1.50. I tell you we felt in clover. We also bought a nice big piece of beef, with lovely suet for puddings, and a big lump of tallow, 25 cents per pound, for candles. Now we are all fixed for housekeeping.

William has traded off his two yoke of cattle for a span of horses and harness, so now we can go when and where we please, and the team will take us to California in the spring, perhaps.

We have now had a heavy snowstorm. The mountains are covered in white. So now that will stop William hauling up the canyon until the snow packs hard. He and two others have been trying today to cut a road through, but they could not. In many places the snow was breast high. They saw five mountain sheep up on the rocks, and could easily have taken them had they had guns. The horns are larger than an ox's. Some young men are going up again tomorrow to try and capture them, as likely they will not wander far away. Bears are frequently seen and killed.

Mr. and Mrs. Hubbard live nine miles back in the mountains. There's a mill up there which he has built. William often sees them, as he goes near there to get his timber.

Pa sent Ma a quantity of music from California, but as we had no piano we all went to Governor Brigham Young's to try it over. He is very friendly indeed. Said William must let him know when we next came to town, as he would invite some musical friends to meet us at his house. The Mormons are glad to get anyone to remain among them, especially if they possess any talent, which they soon found Ma was gifted with.

I have not mentioned dear Sissy. She is not yet weaned, and I guess now I'll have to wait till spring. She don't try to talk any, and has not run about over a month. She has now eight teeth, all cut since she was a year old. She cut her eye teeth first. Wasn't that unusual? She's a darling little ''puss;'' knows all we say to her. I have just made her a black watered silk hood out of that bonnet of mine. You will laugh at it, but when you consider the difficulty of obtaining anything in this far-away valley, you can realize that the

71

folks make their clothing out of anything obtainable. Sissy wears that little red de laine dress, and her little petticoat is from Jimima Parkhurst's cloak. I have saved that nice quilted skirt you gave her, and when weather is colder I shall shorten it for her. Dear little pet; she's a great hand to kiss, and at every meal she has to smack her lips to us; and when the cat is around she toddles off to kiss her. There's a "cat hole" in our door, and she lies down and peeps through it, and clasps her hands and hisses as she sees us do when the mill cattle come near the house. The pretty red saque is still kept for the best, and her long cloak I find very useful. Oh, I wonder how old she will be when you next see her! (A woman grown and married—over twenty years.) William often wishes we were back, and says as soon as he gets any more than he started with he'll be with you. If I were very anxious, I think William would send me back to you in the spring, and he go on alone to California; but it looks best we journey together.

My clothing is very shabby now, as I have had no chance for new since our arrival. That pink calico sunbonnet I have worn on Sundays and week days, and when it looked too mean I made another out of an old lilac calico I brought from England. Rather a contrast to my appearance three or four years previous in London, and I wonder what we should have thought had we foreseen the changes. But I'll make me a black silk hood soon as I get a nice pattern, which will last till we reach the "El Dorado," then I'll not have to dress shabby. Of course, had I known we should winter here, there are several things I left behind which would have been very useful. My cloak, which I gave away, would have done a good service here. It was so pretty, too, and not half worn out, and beautiful material—so much velvet in it. I have nothing to wear now but the green plaid shawl, and that is so fine there's but little warmth in it. Ma loaned me a cloth cloak of hers, but she needed it to make Eddie pants. So now if I am out riding and it gets very cold

I bundle up in a comforter, as many others have to do, and as there's no one here whom I know or care for, my appearance gives me little concern.

William started with a good thick overcoat, and sold it at Kanesville for $3, as he was told there would be no use for it, though there never was a night on the plains but he would have been glad of it. He now uses a waterproof blanket, one Pa bought in Kanesville. There's a hole in the center for his head to go through. This is a Spanish custom or fashion.

Well, I am quite alone just now, as baby is asleep and William is gone to town with Alexander, the mill owner. You write your fruit crop was poor this season. We see nothing but dried apples or peaches, and they are forty cents per pound. We have eight pounds of the latter. How I think of the nice preserves in your cellar just now.

I wonder what you will say at these Mormons building a theater; and it's to be church property. It is to be opened at Christmas. Ma is to be one of the actresses. She is assigned characters in three pieces now rehearsing. She is at present teaching school, but as soon as the Music Hall is finished she will teach music there. Brigham Young has bought a fine English piano, also a melodion, for her use there. John is employed by Brigham in hauling wood from his canyon, which is close by. He is to get $2.50 a day, and Brigham keeps his horses, so he has only to drive to the house, and there a colored man takes the team to the stable; so John likes that. William would like so easy a job, and talks of asking Brigham for one; but I don't like him working in town, I don't like the Mormon influence around him.

The house where Ma lives belongs to a Mormon who has three wives. He has just gone to England en route to Prussia ''on a mission,'' as they term it, and the day before he left he married a widow, so that makes four. The other night William and I went to a party. There were some young ladies present. I enquired of the hostess who they were. She replied they were her husband's wife's children! How strange it did seem.

Well, this letter is long enough, and I had best conclude, though you may not get it before spring, as the mails are so delayed on account of snow. Still, they leave each month, and go as far as Fort Bridger. Give lots of love to Uncle and his family. Beg them to write me.

With much love to you both, from yours ever,

SISTER LUCY.

This letter is finished on the 27th of November, 1852, having been in hand over five weeks.

LETTER NUMBER EIGHT.

Great Salt Lake, Utah Territory, January 30, 1853.

DEAREST SISTER. IT SEEMS SO LONG SINCE I HEARD from you that I get very uneasy, and wonder if any letters have been sent and not reached me. I have only just concluded to write you, and shall have to hurry somewhat, or this will not be in time for the next mail. I cannot now write a very satisfactory letter, as I feel in constant excitement about leaving here. Oh, how I wish I could be back again with you. I am sick at heart of this Mormon country, though I dare not thus express myself to oursiders, for we Gentiles seem to be under surveillance constantly, and might not fare so well as we do (and that's poor enough) were we to express our true feelings.

Mr. and Mrs. Hubbard, whom we used to board with in Moline, have been sharing our little log cabin with us for the past two months, since my last was written, and they will remain with us until we start for California. You may guess we are pretty crowded. We have two bedsteads, each with only one leg, as they are only slats laying on poles driven in the side of the cabin wall. But they answer very well, though when we all are up and around we can scarce turn around. Mr. and Mrs. Hubbard lived about nine miles up the canyon, the same where William has had to haul his shingle timber from, till the snow fell so deep it was no longer safe to remain there. So we offered them our cabin to share, and it's well they accepted, or their lives might have been lost.

After they left their shanty, some men went up there to cut timber, and occupied a cabin close by Hubbard's. One day the wind was blowing very hard, causing the fireplace to smoke, so they concluded to go into Hubbard's shanty to bake some bread, and were thus engaged, when a terrific noise was heard approaching, which proved to be a snow-slide or avalanche down the mountain side, burying the cabin, not leaving a sign of a dwelling.

There were three men in the company, but one had just stepped outside, and was walking down the path, when he heard the tremendous crash and roar, and on looking back saw what happened; and fearing for the lives of his companions, he ran to a mill two-and-a-half miles distant and obtained help to return and dig for his two companions. They labored hard, and at length found one man quite dead, apparently killed instantly by the falling of a rock which partly formed the fireplace. The poor man was just turning the bread when the summons came.

They continued to dig for some hours, but could find no trace of the other man. But at length a sound or call was noticed; but it was so faint under the snow, and gave no intimation from whence it came. Up to this time they had been digging in the cabin, which they uncovered. Now they left it and began outside, and worked there an hour or two, but returned to the cabin, and after a long search came to a boot. They moved the foot, and, oh joy! it moved again. Poor man, he was pinned down full length, his arms extended over his head, and so he had lain six hours. One of the cabin poles was across his hands, so he was pinned, with no chance to move after he was first knocked down. Poor fellow, he was sensible all the time, but thought his last hour had come. The men did their utmost to revive him, and made haste to the valley for a team to bring him and the corpse out. William took his horses next day and brought them down. The young man was unable to work for some weeks, but has now recovered.

They belonged to a company from Farmington, Illinois, on their way to California, but remained (like ourselves) and were engaged to put up a mill in the canyon under Mr. Hubbard's superintendence. The man who was killed left a wife and five children in Farmington. Oh, what sad news to send back!

There are frequent snowslides when wind is high, and sometimes I get so uneasy when William is gone up there. One day he barely escaped a slide as he was driving up, for one came down just ahead of his horses, and all traces of a road being covered in deep snow, he had to return home. (I might mention that when William went up in the canyon with his team, as mentioned on preceding page, to recover the man from the avalanche, he was accompanied by one Porter Rockwell, a noted Mormon called a "Danite," or "Destroying Angel," he being then and in after years one of Brigham's emissaries when any persons objectionable were desired out of the way. And many are the crimes laid up against him done in the interest of Mormonism.

This man was an acquaintance of Alexander's, whom William was employed by at the mill. So we often saw him around, and perhaps it was to our interest to treat him with cordiality, for doubtless we, as Gentiles (therefore objectionable) were under his surveillance. I used to watch him with a certain awe, though scarce knowing why, except that he was "Porter Rockwell," and must be treated as one in power—for evil if not for good deeds. He had the fashion of wearing long hair, like a woman's, behind, and having it braided in a coil at the nape of his neck. I now wonder what could have been my feelings when my loved husband left me to go up in that dreary canyon with his team and none other than "Porter Rockwell" for his companion. Doubtless a kind Providence watched over my loved one, but it seemed a risk some might not dare to run in those days, for all immigrants were in more or less danger among the Mormons.

But at this time, after passing a winter of hardship among them, all the talk among us Gentiles was about leaving for California, for we all are so tired of this Salt Lake Valley, and we wish to be among the first who leave, which time is expected to be early in March.)

Mr. and Mrs. Hubbard have engaged their passage through with a family named Greeley; he and his son-in-law, a Mr. Rogers, are millers by trade, and fortunately have had steady employ in a flouring mill most of the winter, and have lived out at the mill in comfortable circumstances compared to most other immigrants; consequently their outfit for the overland trip was better than most of us could obtain. They are a genial, pleasant family; Christians withal, and what satisfaction I feel when in their company, and no objectionable Mormon doctrines are thrust upon us. But we have to be very watchful in our doings and sayings at all times, and how I long to be again in a free country, before Porter Rockwell is put on my or our trail! We could not, however, make satisfactory arrangements with the Greeley family, and so I expect we may start with our own wagon if William can meet with some man to accompany us and help drive and do chores, and then take our chances of joining some company on the road after we have started.

Since the above was written Mr. Greeley has called, and seems to think some way can be arranged for us to go in his company. Oh, what a pleasant trip then I should look forward to. They expect to be four months on the road, as they will have to remain perhaps four or five weeks in Carson Valley, till the Sierra Nevada Mountains can be crossed. But when there, plenty of employment can be found at gold mining. Oh, don't I look forward to this Land of Promise, this "El Dorado," as the Spanish term it.

I have not seen Ma since Christmas Day. We rode into town then to see them all. But some way I cannot feel the same cordiality since Ma has joined the Mormons, and also become a stage actress. Their theater is in full operation now, and Ma is in constant demand, both for her musical talent and her acting abilities. You know I have never attended a theatrical performance in my life, but since Ma has joined the company here, I cannot well refuse to go at her invitation, and so the other day we were all invited to spend the afternoon at Brigham Young's (and of course no one would refuse such an invitation). We were to meet some musical folks, and then all go to the theater to spend the evening. We had a very pleasant time indeed. It was such a treat to us all, after "roughing it" for so many months, to be guests in a nicely appointed, (and to us) elegant home, with all the luxuries of civilization around us. Mrs. Young (Brigham's first wife) was the hostess, and a very homelike, pleasant woman she appeared. We saw nothing of any of the other wives, they being kept in a row of little cottages near by (for future reference). We spent the afternoon and early evening in music and song, Mr. Dunbar, a noted English singer, being present. My little Sarah began to be troublesome toward evening, so the Governor kindly ordered his carriage, and Lilly took the baby home to bed, so we all could enjoy the theater performance, which of course I was interested in, though as it was part tragedy (I think they called it), and I could only see the humorous side, which kept me on the broad grin, and every time William would look at me he seemed annoyed at my want of appreciation, and that made me "grin" the more.

The piece was "The Spaniards in Peru." There's a hand-to-hand encounter in it, which amused me, as I could see one man hit his opponent by accident, causing his nose to bleed, and this, of course, must not then be noticed. So I laughed at that, and then William got mad. Then there was a vestal scene, and a tribe of young virgins (?) chanting solemnly with their crucifixes, and marching. As Ma and Mrs. Grimshaw were among their number (for their fine voices), I just laughed at the whole performance, though I hope I did not disturb any one. But William said I certainly was proof against tragedy that evening. I hope Brigham never heard of my lack of appreciation.

The Mormons are great for parties, especially in winter, and William and I have attended several, as a good supper is a great inducement to any of us emigrants. I was engaged to write ball tickets for one party, and thus earned a trifle. The Mormons open their balls with prayer, which to me seems a strange blending. What would our London friends think! But this is a strange community, and I long to leave it, indeed I do.

When the Hubbards came from the canyon they had two nice little pigs they were fattening for their food on the road. But as they hired their passage with the Greeleys they did not need them, so we killed one the other morning before breakfast. It was such a treat as we had been without meat for some time. This, of course, seems strange to you, and would to us had we not become accustomed to a vegetable diet, and being always hungry, too, it matters little what we have so long as we get enough of any kind. It all tastes good, and we shall reach California in due time.

We are trying to sell anything of clothing we can spare, as much to lighten our load as to furnish things more necessary. William sold his best coat for 400 pounds of flour. It was lucky he had one to sell, though he was glad to have it to wear the afternoon we spent at the Governor's. But poor man, his shoes were all worn out, and he had worn moccasins for some time, as they could always be obtained of the Indians. But shoes were too great a luxury for emigrants to purchase, i.e., a nice shoe. Fortunately he borrowed a pair for the occasion of an emigrant. Oh, it's laughable the contrivances one and all submit to on this trip. My nice satin dress, which came from England, several women have been so anxious to barter for. I offered it to one woman for a good cow, which would be a great help on our journey, but she would not make the trade. But finally Mrs. Alexander, the mill man's wife, took it in exchange for an overcoat of her husband's, which William could wear all the time and badly needed, and also a dress pattern (woollen material), which was easier to pack in my little trunk than a good silk dress was, as I was always afraid of some accident to it when we were on the road last season. I still have my black brocaded dress like yours, so that is sufficient for all present or rather future occasions.

William had a new pair of suspenders which he brought from the States, and did not need. A young man was very anxious to get them. Asked the price: Six bits. He took them, but enquired if William would want all the pay down, then! Oh, these Mormons are a hardup crowd, and money is seldom seen.

At Christmas a box of things came from Pa in California. To Ma he sent a rich brocade silk dress pattern, some silk velvet for a bonnet, ribbons, gloves, etc., and also gloves for me, and a gold dollar for each member of the family, so I guess he is doing pretty well. Our two dollars we had to spend for meat, and baby's for a pair of shoes, though I hated to part with our gifts so soon. But perhaps it was lucky we had even that much (or little, you may say) to get what we most needed. We have been without tea or sugar for some time, but William got a store order for $6, so we gladly exchanged it for tea, coffee and sugar, and thus we are helped along, and time passes rapidly, and we'll soon be leaving. Oh, how different I hope to find things in California.

Brigham wished to see William before he left, to give him his blessing, according to a custom they have. He also prophesied that

William and I should join their church, and that Lillie would live to see the coming of Christ. We have our doubts of the fulfillment of these prophesies.

Well, I may write again before we start on our journey, which will be in four or five weeks, I hope. I had such a time trying to get a pair of shoes for baby, and at length had to cut the tops off a pair of men's boots and get a shoemaker to make them. He charged a dollar. But there were no babies' shoes in the stores.

Dearest Sister, farewell till we meet, and I trust we shall meet again in this world.

Lovingly yours,

LUCY COOKE.

LETTER NUMBER NINE.

Salt Lake City, Utah Territory, March 12, 1853.

MY DEAR SISTER: I AM WITH MA PAYING HER A LAST visit preparatory to leaving California. She has just received quite a budget of letters from Pa, amongst which was a letter from Pa to William and one for me containing a letter from Uncle dated September 7, 1852, though it contained no particular news, as he doubted if I should ever receive it.

I wrote you some two months ago but it is so uncertain when letters will reach you, on account of snow. Still, I wished you to know when we started; and oh, we are so rejoiced the time has come, being so tired of our sojourn here.

Pa writes he is very anxious to have all the family come on. He has a good position and is doing well. His employers wish his family to join him, and they promise to do great things for us all. I guess Ma will go, but not till July or August, as she has just commenced giving music lessons, so she will have to finish the quarter. Pa wants William there much, as there's a fine chance for him to take management of a farm belonging to merchants in the city. Pa has entire charge of everything, and does as he thinks best in general managing. He says he found the chickens getting pretty numerous about the farm, so he took 150 to the city, for which he got $300, and $2.50 per dozen for the eggs. Flour was selling at $50 per 100! He says he never before witnessed so much wealth and poverty side by side as is to be seen in San Francisco. His letter is dated San Francisco, December 29, 1852. I will give an extract from his letter, showing his kindness of heart for his loved ones at this season. He writes:

> I have thought of all the loved ones, big and little, that I left in the valley of the mountains, almost constantly the last few days, as Christmas has always been a happy time with me in the bosom of my family; and the enjoyment of all, especially the children, on Christmas Eve when hanging up the stockings for the visit of Santa Claus, and the opening of them next morning, to empty them of their treasures, in past seasons, were vividly presented before my mind in rapid review, far back into the past, so as almost to make me realize them again. etc.

Then he goes on to tell of his engagement and the one awaiting for us, "either of which, if rightly managed, would make a snug fortune in from three to five years." Ain't that a pleasant outlook for us, after the hardships of this valley?

But I must return to ourselves. We have paid our passage through with a family who, like us, remained here this winter. We give them a yoke of oxen and wagon for our two selves and $20 for Sissy, and William is to drive two-thirds of the distance. I shall have nothing to do but mind Sissy, so I think we shall be more comfortable than last season. We have a wide track wagon, with projections at the sides. Our bed is the whole width, and will remain all day as at night, so we can lie down whenever disposed. Mr. and Mrs. Hubbard go in same company. We are to be taken to Sacramento City, and then shall have to take steamboat to San Francisco. We must remain in Carson Valley four or five weeks till the mountains are passable.

Doubtless we shall have an anxious trip before us, and then there's considerable danger from Indians when nearing Humboldt. Our men are all well armed. William carries a brace of pistols and a bowie knife. Ain't that blood-curdling! Hope he won't hurt himself.

I am thankful to say we are in excellent health, and have been all winter, though we never lived so frugal. But everything we did get was eaten with such relish always. I have gained seventeen pounds in weight since on the Missouri River. Ma and I each weighed then 115 pounds. Now I weigh 132. Dear Sarah weighs 28 pounds, so she is pretty chunky. She still sucks here two fingers. I have just cut up that nice green skirt you gave me to make her a petticoat. It is so nice and warm for the little pet. Oh, how often I wish you could see her; she is getting so cunning. But if we all are spared a few years you will see us all back, for it is our fixed desire and intention to return. (Alas, we never did.)

I have been very busy preparing for our journey. Have pulled my three comforters to pieces and washed them. You will remember they were lined with white muslin, or rather unbleached. This I have taken for sheets, and am using the comfort you made before I was married. The red flannel binding has been useful in several ways. It seems so nice to have sweet, clean bedding again, though of course it soon gets dingy when we are on the road, though I wash whenever I get any chance and my first sheet washing was done on "The Plains," with none other chance for drying than over a wagon wheel. So you can judge of the success.

I have sold my satin dress to get William an overcoat. It is a very nice one; heavy broadcloth, nicely lined and silk bound; in fact, it's much too good for our need, but he had to have one, and my frock was only in my way, and I can soon get another when we reach California. I got a new figured alpacca dress besides the coat, which the lady paid $1.25 per yard for, and it will be a good second best dress when we reach our journey's end.

My pretty black silk is about done for, as I wore it considerably in the city through the winter.

I am delighted to learn our boxes, which were shipped around the Horn, have arrived in San Francisco. Pa had to pay $50 freight. My sea chest had the padlock broken off, and a stick was run through the hasp, but Pa thought nothing had been disturbed. My china suffered some. Two of the cups, one saucer and a glass salt cellar were all that were broken. How I long to get my things again. It seems an age since they left us, but it may yet be long before I can see them. I presume Pa will store them somewhere till our arrival in the Promised Land.

We have all been twice to the Governor lately, and I assure you we were well treated. Ma wished us to go and bid him good-bye before we left. He has loaned Ma one of his pianos, a very handsome one. She already has several pupils, and having the Governor's daughters will be a good recommendation to others.

I am so disappointed in having no letters from you, as now there's no chance till we reach San Francisco, which may be four long months.

March 22d. Dearest Marianne: We are expecting to leave to-day. It's beautiful weather. We have been out visiting every day for two weeks. William went to bid President Young good-bye yesterday. He gave him his blessing, and said we would prosper. So that's encouraging, from such high authority. We have met with much kindness among the Mormons, and shall always have reason to speak well of them. I must conclude, though I might continue this letter and still interest you.

Ma has been unwilling to have us start on such a journey without some chance to get a light in the night, in the event of either of us being sick. What could we do in the dark? I told you, I think, that no candles were to be found for sale anywhere, there being no tallow in the city. So folks had to sit by firelight or in darkness through the past winter. Ma went around among her lady friends and secured five candles. Thin as rushlights they were, but they seem priceless, almost, to us. She also got me a small phial of essence of peppermint for sickness. So now I feel ready for emergencies, day or night.

I have just made me a cloth sacque, and lined it with a blanket, so I shall take comfort in it, for we expect some very cold weather. Sissy is waking, so I can write no more, except to assure you of my constant love.

Good bye.

SISTER LUCY.

LETTER NUMBER TEN.

This letter commenced the latter part of April, 1853.

MY DEAR MARIANNE: AS I AM AGAIN ON THE ROAD I shall try to give you an account of our travels, though I doubt if I do so as regularly as I did last season. We left Salt Lake on the 31st of March though this you will know ere now, as I mailed a letter on that day to our Uncle.

We have now been on the road about three weeks, one of which we laid by, as we were on good food, and no use to hurry, seeing we cannot cross the Goose Creek Mountains (on account of snow) for some weeks. I have very much enjoyed being out on the road again and among Gentiles. We had rather anxious times getting started, as several young men in our company had made themselves obnoxious to the Mormons, and we feared they might be waylaid and returned to the city. We were all closely watched, and so we gladly made distance between our camp and the Mormon city. One man they hunted after, but he was hidden away and kept quiet till miles had been passed.

We are now in Mr. Greeley's company, and so far enjoy ourselves. We live first rate, and it's so nice to have women folks manage the cooking; things look so much sweeter. I don't know that they have any better food or more variety than Pa did last year, but it looks better. Tonight for supper we had fried sausage, eggs, boiled cabbage, bread, butter and tea, milk, etc. It's so nice to have plenty of the latter, also butter and eggs. The women folks have been saving these for some time previous to starting. We have a few potatoes, also, though they will not last long. But perhaps other things than our food will be interesting. We have a very comfortable, roomy wagon all to ourselves; we enjoy that, I assure you. The loading is under the bed, and but two meat barrels in front, which have clean flat lids, making nice tables. Then there's room to move about comfortably. Oh, how different to the crowded manner we were last season. Still, the main point is not so good as then, i.e., the cattle. Pa had very fine teams, and plenty of them, and now these folks have very light cattle, and mostly cows, and they in poor condition from hard winter. Our wagon, though a heavy one, has only two yoke, one of oxen and one of cows. All Pa's wagons had four yoke last year. The passengers in our company doubt if we can get through with the four wagons.

We crossed Bear River last week on a little raft of nine small logs. There's always a ferry there during the season; but we were very early this year, and no ferry started. So our men folks agreed to cut logs and make their own raft, which would take on just one wagon at a time.

There had now several other companies joined us, and twenty or thirty wagons awaited crossing. The cattle all had to swim over. This was a very tedious affair, for poor brutes, they are so unwilling to take the water, and this stream was very wide now.

I met with a little episode which might have proved serious at the crossing. When our wagon was put on the raft it was thought I might as well go over at the same time; not inside, as that was deemed dangerous. So I was told to stand by a hind wheel, with baby in my arms. The raft was let loose from shore, but owing to the wagon not being pushed in the center of the raft, it backed off into the water, sending the raft and some portion of my legs under water. Of course I was much scared, as the jerk made my baby fall back over my arm. I thought my child was gone. I screamed, "Oh, my child!" But William, who was on with us, threw his arm around my back and caught her, and held us both tight to the wheel until the raft was dragged back to shore. The folks said I showed good courage, as some women would have yelled the whole time. The hind part of our wagon was under water, but we hoped the contents had not suffered, and again it was placed on the raft and was safely taken over, though I remained to go in the skiff belonging to the ferry, as it had been discovered hidden away on an island from last season's service.

Well, at length we all crossed safely, but could not get the cattle to swim over, though they twice had been driven into the river. Poor things, they all crowded up in bunches, and seemed so frightened, whilst thirty or forty men were shouting and whipping and throwing dirt and stones at them. But all in vain, for they would not swim over, and as night was coming on, they were let come out of the water and remain that side until the next morning. They were then again driven in, and after a long time finally swam across.

We then thought our troubles over for a while, but we soon came to another stream, which our guide book said was bridged, but we found the stream a wide river and no bridge visible. So another consultation was held, and it was agreed to remove our wagon bed and send the running gear back to Bear River for a skiff.

While they were gone I thought it a good chance to clear out my wagon and see if anything got wet the night before. When lo, on opening my box I found everything soaked with water! I cried with vexation, but finally took out everything and hung them around on bushes to dry. There were nice clean towels and English tablecloths, wringing wet and stained our clothing. Sissy's white clothes, which I was carefully saving for our final destination in California, were ruined until all washed and again ironed. But all this was only another of the many episodes of the journey.

But to return to the stream crossing, which in our guide book is named the worst for mud on all the journey. The skiff arrived, wagons were emptied of heaviest articles, they being sent in the skiff, and a man undertook to wade or swim the river, and thus ascertain its depths. He managed to wade pretty well, the water not coming higher than his armpits in its deepest places. The poor cattle were again made to ford or swim, and the men drew the wagons partly across, where the bridge was found, and thus by using poles and feeling their way William and five or six other men waded from noon till sundown taking the wagons about half way over, where a man with a yoke of oxen was wading the other side to draw them out. Then was the job of loading all the wagons again. Oh, surely we are seeing the elephant, from the tip of his trunk to the end of his tail! I wish you could have seen the men in the water. The noises they made seemed to indicate a pleasant pastime. But I was thankful when it was all over and we were under way again.

May 1st. It is now a long time since I began this, during which we have left Mr. Greeley's company and joined one which had traveled near us for some time, a Mr. Holly being the proprietor of this company. We left Mr. Greeley's company because they expected William to do the camp duties such as gathering wood and fetching water every night. This he would not do, as what he had paid for our passage was ample to secure such chores being done for us. William helped with milking and took his turn in churning, but this did not seem to satisfy Greeley, so William drew out his wagon and yoke of cattle and joined this Holly company. I don't think I shall enjoy the change socially, for these new folks seem not the class I care to mingle with, so we shall keep to ourselves and our wagon. Mrs. Holly seems to be bossing it over the men folks, so I guess I'll not make her acquaintance. She's not my style, I soon see that.

So far as teams are concerned, we have made an excellent change, the man we are now with having a fine lot of cattle as could be desired. He brought them through to Salt Lake last season from Chicago. Oh, they are pictures, in such fine physical condition. Then he has loose cattle, which is a great advantage, being never obliged to work any but those fit to travel. Mr. Greeley's company could only travel very slow, the cows being so poor, and oh, such a time we have had at a mudhole or a hill. But Mr. Holly concluded to leave them, as we can out-travel them every day.

Our company now consists of six wagons, thirty-seven head of cattle and three horses. Mrs. Holly rides in a light horse wagon, as we did last year. Directly we joined this company Holly put three yoke of fine cattle on our wagon, which is only lightly laden, having but five sacks of flour besides our bed and clothing. I assure you it is somewhat different to riding behind cows. Why, we travel right along, through mud, over mountains, snow, or anything that happens to come next. So, as I before said, so far as teams are concerned (and surely that's the main thing) we have made a happy change. But we live very poorly. The bacon is awful—so musty—and no vegetables; nothing but bacon, bread, and dishcloth coffee! Oh, how I missed the milk and butter that Greeleys had. William has tried around the camp and has got a cow to milk and has the milk for his trouble, so as long as its owner travels with us I shall have plenty. And now I have five pounds of butter, which is choice as gold. I got it of Greeleys when we left them. I should not have been thus favored, but I happened to have a pair of new leather shoes I bought in the valley for three dollars, and as one of their women folks was near barefoot, they were glad

93

to make the trade. So they paid the half in butter at 30 cents per pound, and the accomodation was mutual, for I did not need the shoes.

I think I told you or wrote in Uncle's letter that there were three single men in our first company, one of whom being the man the Mormons were hunting for when we left Salt Lake. Well, they have joined this company, for the sake of traveling faster. They are all pleasant fellows. But Holly's crowd seem to quarrel considerably. Sometimes I think there will be a fight, and I get awfully scared. Holly told one tall, lanky chap he'd cut him in two and make bridge timbers out of him! That struck me as a novel idea.

We crossed Goose Creek Mountains about nine days ago. Had to double teams through some of the snowdrifts. But we got over in one day without so much difficulty, though one or two ascents were almost perpendicular. My wagon seemed as though it stood on end. But I rode all the time, for it was a very disagreeable day, and snowing fast and wind blowing in gales. However, when we got down in the valley it was quite pleasant weather, but on looking back at the mountains the snow was falling fast up there. Last Friday it snowed so hard, and we were then on a plain and lost our road; couldn't tell which direction we were to go. But the ground was white with snow, and no wood but sagebrush, and that a long way off. Oh, it was so cheerless. So we all three went to bed to keep warm. The cattle, by nosing around in the snow for feed, found grass called "crazy grass," and sure enough, it did turn them crazy. The men all had to be around and work with them during the night, giving them slices of our rancid bacon, grease being an antidote for poison. I was not sorry to know the bacon was being disposed of, though I wondered what we should have in its place.

With the exception of two wagons, which have gone ahead to

establish a ferry on the Humboldt, we are the first company on the road, though there's plenty behind us. Today being Sunday we have camped for the day, not because 'tis Sunday, but there's good feed. There's another company camped in sight, with 1000 head of sheep, so we shall try to keep ahead of them. We meet Indians every day now, and today a party of them are camped on the opposite side of the creek. They all seem friendly, though. We try to trade for their buckskins, but they will only exchange for "caribee," i.e., guns or ammunition.

May 14th. I am not very regular in writing our travels, but it's getting an old story, and one day is as another, after so many weeks and months. We have now been traveling on the Humboldt some days; the weather is much warmer, quite hot at noon. We have seen eight or ten graves the last day or two, so suppose it's unhealthy in hot weather. One grave we passed was that of a young man shot by an Indian while on guard, so the board at his grave informed us. He lived two days, it says. I wish I had taken his name and date.

We have seen but few of this new tribe, "Diggers." They are very shy, and keep hid in the willows along the banks of the river. It gives me a strange feeling to have them so near, as they might take a shot at some of us. We saw three apparently watching us, so our men folks tried to coax them to come over, and bread was thrown in the water as an inducement for them to swim over. After long waiting they came, and rather put some of us modest females to the blush, they being naked with the exception of a "breech clout." Oh, but they were ugly creatures. Very retreating foreheads and no eyebrows. When they found we were friendly they followed us some miles and took dinner with us. We had an idea that it might benefit us if we could get an Indian to travel with us a day or two, whilst we seemed in their haunts or localities. So some of the men folks tried to make our wishes known, and one fellow signified his willingness by coming along and eating any food given him, so seeming on friendly terms. The first day he was with us it rained very hard, so we could not travel, and the men folks were lounging around idle in the tents, Mr. Indian among the rest. Some objected to his presence, on closer acquaintance finding certain nameless little insects infested his person, and therefore he was not a desirable "companion de voyage." But the men were lacking amusement, and one suggested it might be a benefit were the Indian subjected to a "tobacco shampoo" and haircut. So at it they went in true barber style, and all hands seemed satisfied with their morning's work. Mr. Indian was rather dumpish; possibly the strong tobacco water had got in its work. But so long as the rain came down the fellow kept inside the tent, back of the little stove. But the rain ceased, and we prepared to travel, feeling we had one good Indian to pilot us awhile. But he had left, and our men were one gun the fewer, for "Lo" had absconded, and thus the cleaning process was of no avail but to cause merriment whenever mentioned.

Yesterday we had to camp soon after starting, for a cow calved, and today we have come about eight miles, and have again stopped for same cause, but suppose we shall go in two or three hours. The calves are to be carried in the wagons for two or three days. We crossed the bridge built by the men who had gone ahead of us some time ago. William paid for our wagon going over, as Mr. Holly was going to ferry the stream, using one of the wagon beds for a boat, but as that leaked so much and such risk of our clothing getting wet, we preferred paying the toll of the bridge, which was very reasonable, the ferryman charging us but $1, as we paid it ourselves, the usual toll being $3. Mr. Holly gave William 75 cents towards it. He also had to treat his men with $5 worth of whiskey for going in the water, and they dropped a sack of sugar, 100 pounds, so he would have done better had he paid the toll and gone on without delay of a day's time.

There were a number of Indians around at this place, and I had a good chance to trade for a fur or two. I swapped one of my small blankets for a pretty robe of prairie dog skins. I think there are ten in it, all nicely sewed together. My blanket was considerably worn. I wonder the Indian was willing to trade. But they always seem so glad to get hold of a blanket. Another Indian had some beautiful mink skins tied over his shoulder and under his arm, with some kind of a bag for his arrows. It took my fancy (the skins, I mean) as being just enough to make a nice flat boa. William at the time had on an old flannel shirt, and being a warm day, he was in his shirt sleeves. I called him to me whilst the Indian stood by, and I went through the sign language intimating my desire to trade the shirt for the skins. He seemed to consent, so I made William strip off his shirt then and there and pass it over to the Indian, and I got the skins.

Well, a young man in our company, seeing my desire for furs presented me with a very fine wildcat skin, he having just traded for several, so I have a nice collection and am quite proud of them. I found on looking them over that vermin were quite plenty in them, so I could not have them inside our wagon. I tied them in sacks underneath, and thus they passed through several creeks or streams, and were finally cleansed. The catskin will make a pretty muff, as it's such beautiful, long, soft fur. I suppose the squaws do the tanning.

Oh, what dreadful places we have had to go through lately. The mud at the banks of the forks of the Humboldt was so deep that at one place nine yoke of our cattle had to be put on one wagon, and then it was a dreadful pull, and chains broke pretty fast. Yesterday William called me out of my wagon to come and see an ox down in the mud. Nothing was visible but the top of his back and head; his nose even was covered. Almost every week and sometimes twice we have to put boards across on the projections and put all the loading on them, for the streams we cross come quite a piece up our wagon box. But every stream we cross brings us nearer our journey's end, and we all are getting tired of the trip. Oh, what a loss I am at for amusement as I ride along. I could knit, but I have only some red yarn, which I bought for Sis, but it's too near summer to commence woollen socks. if I only had some muslin, how nice I could be preparing for our underclothes, for we each are quite destitute. I have no nightdress at all, so sleep in a colored sacque. Sissy now wears a little red flannel dress I made out of that piece you saw. She also wears that green quilted skirt, and on warm days they are too heavy. But I have no fears for the future, as Pa will see we have all we need when we reach him. It seems quite providential he went on to California last season, as we feel we have a home and something to expect.

Oh, if I could but see you, my loved sister, and have a long talk together, how happy I should feel. I shall look forward to such a season as not unlikely. My earnest desire is that we may end our days near each other, and I think we shall.

We are now over the desert, the forty-mile desert of which we had heard much, consequently we dreaded it. The evening before we reached it we camped very early, and had supper and let the cattle feed good, and toward night all was started again, as we were to cross it in the night for the sake of coolness. Every one filled their tin canteens with water at the last camping place, but the water was very poor (brackish); but there was no other well. Sis and I went to bed at dark, as usual, but the men folks were all walking, and expected so to do most of the night. The sand was very deep, and the wagons dragged along slowly. Toward midnight it began to rain, and the oxen showed signs of exhaustion, and what little water we carried was given to those most in need. Mr. Holly began to fear our wagon, which was the largest and heaviest in the crowd, could not be hauled any farther, and that some change must be made or he would get stuck on the desert. A consultation was held, and William came and awoke me, telling me that I would have to get out and go in one of the other wagons, as Holly would haul ours no farther. I was just all broken up at this bad news, for our roomy wagon had been our pride and comfort. But as we had given it to Holly in part payment for our passage, it was his, and he must do as suited him best. So I bundled up myself and baby, and the men gathered up the bedding and all the traps and threw in other wagons, wherever there happened to be any room, and I tumbled in anywhere. No more good bed for us, but just a chance to exist in among the pork barrels and all the dirt of men's old clothes. But there was no help for us, and I had to suffer the inconvenience of the change. Perhaps I did not cry, but I think I did. But there was this comfort, we should soon reach the Carson River.

Well, our good wagon was left on the desert. But such was the prevailing custom on the Plains, to destroy anything that you might not then need, and so prevent the next one from benefiting by your discarded property, whatever it might be. Perhaps I ought not to write that this custom was general, for it was not; but some would do so, and Holly was of that class. He therefore had our nice good wagon set fire to, and when we left there was a big bonfire blazing. It did seem a "burning" shame, for surely some eimgrant might have benefited by its use.

We reached the Carson river in the early forenoon, having traveled the whole night. Teams and men pretty well jaded. We found a shanty or two and several tents here, and the place was given the not inappropriate name of "Rag Town," for such described the appearance of most of the emigrant arrivals. Refreshments were here to be had for man and beast, whiskey seeming a staple article for the former. A family named Fuller, who came across the Plains the previous summer, had a little trading post here, and strange to say we recognized one of Pa's wagon covers with his name, thus, "William Cooke, Dubuque Co., Iowa, No. 4." We did not learn how it came there, but possibly Pa sold his outfit or a portion when he reached California the previous season, and some of these people might have purchased.

Our travel now with Mr. Holly's company was about through and as the mountains were not free enough from snow for travel, we had to halt awhile, and the following short note will explain our situation:

Carson Valley, June 5, 1853.

Dearest Sister: We arrived here about one week ago, and shall be detained here until the early part of July, not being able to cross the Sierra Nevada Mountains with wagons. William has hired out to mine (in what is now called Gold Canyon in the town of Dayton). He is to receive $50 per month and board, that itself being $2 per day. I am helping round the house of William's employer, a man named McMartin. I get my own and Sissy's board for pay. The place is a tavern and trading post, and being the first we reach after the long journey, everyone stops here, and pack trains from Sacramento arrive frequently, and thus we get the news of the outside world. Mrs. McMartin is a pleasant young woman, and I enjoy helping her in her work, and the board is excellent, such a treat to us.

This is a great rendezvous for gamblers. Cards are being played day and night and William sometimes stays up all night in charge of the store. They all make a great pet of Sis, she being the only child staying here. The Carson river is back of the log house, and sometimes I take my baby and we bathe among the willows, where the sand makes a pleasant footing for us. We sleep in a wagon standing near the dwelling, and I enjoy the situation and surroundings quite well. There are twenty boarders here, most of them mining for Mr. McMartin up the canyon. Each night the pans containing the black sand and gold are brought to the store, and there washed in big tubs or half barrels. This is our first introduction to gold mining. There's a little creek of clear water across the road, and sometimes I go and pick up clear, pretty rocks; in some, gold is plainly seen. I have a chance to send this long letter to Sacramento to mail, and must close. We are all well. Kindest love to yourself and dear husband. From your loving sister,

LUCY COOKE.

(Whilst staying at McMartin's we got acquainted with a young man living there named George Ruggles. He took a great fancy to my little Sis, and she would toddle after him every time she saw him, and would watch him milk the cows of an evening. After we left Carson Valley this same young man opened a little trading store or wayside post near the foot of the trail over the Sierras, and the following summer was murdered by a desperado named "Mickey Free," who was afterward convicted and hanged in Coloma, Eldorado county, in the early fifties. A sigh we breathed to the memory of poor George Ruggles.)

We remained in Carson Valley one month, and then paid our passage through to California, to a Dr. Pingree, who was taking his train through to Marysville, his final destination. His was a pleasant company, and we were glad to be of his party, it being a great contrast to the Holly crowd, with which we had arrived at Carson Valley. I sent my last journal to my sister by some packers whom we met a short distance out of Carson Valley, and as luck would have it, they were carrying letters for emigrants stopping at McMartin's station among which was one for us from Ma, with the intelligence that Pa had gone to Australia! Judge of our disappointment to find, instead of having a good home and friends to go to in San Francisco, we were destitute of either, and with but little means.

Of course I had a long cry as we traveled along, but we talked over our situation, and decided to remain at Hangtown and try our success there, it being the first town on our route over the mountains. We camped our first night in a pleasant spot since called Genoa, and then journeyed on to Lake Valley, at the foot of the Sierra Nevada range, which we now had to cross. We camped the night in this valley, and all our thoughts and conversation were on the morrow's labor, which would take us over the summit and into the Promised Land. It was decided that each and all of our company must climb the mountains a-foot and all the bedding and supplies were packed on the loose horses in the train. Each woman had to take charge of her young ones. There were but few in the party, however, and I had my Sissy to care for. The empty wagons were considered load sufficient for the poor cattle.

Everything being in readiness, an early start was made next morning, and a wagon was started to lead the way up the mountain trail. The women folks went along single file to pick their easiest route over and around the rocks and boulders. I carried along a bucket of bread and milk for my own and baby's lunch, and the toilsome journey was begun. Some places the rocks were so large I had to climb up, place my baby ahead, lift up my bucket, and then drag myself. Thus I toiled for an hour or two, and finally sat down to eat my lunch in preference to carrying it further. Then up and up again, many a weary step, and how I thought of loved friends away back; but the feeling that soon we should be in California gave strength and new courage. It took the whole morning for us to gain the summit, where the wagon had arrived ahead of us who were on foot. The men who accompanied it had now to return down the mountain trail to assist with other wagons. From the summit we stood and gazed with wonder and delight, and lo, in the distance could we see water gleaming in the sunshine. It was Lake Bigler, or Tahoe, as it was afterward called. Sure, we were now in California! And our trials would soon be of the past, whilst the future, oh, where was its limit?

The two or three men who were about to leave us women folks for a few hours, whilst they returned to the valley for the other wagons, left the cattle all staked out safely, so we might have no disturbance during their absence, and we could sleep or lounge around for hours without fear. Among the cattle first brought up were two bulls used as leaders, and named after two Mormon dignitaries, viz., "Brigham" and "Heber C." (Kimball). These animals, after eating the surrounding grass and anxious for more, had broken the ropes which tied "Brigham," and he got loose. They both were rather vicious beasts, and given to battle when any chance occurred. So when we women folks saw the animal loose and no man around, fear and terror filled our fertile imaginations of the possibilities awaiting us, and who knew but we all might be killed before anyone could come to our help. A horrified consultation among us women ensued, and on one of the biggest boulders we all scrambled, to be ready for the gory battle soon as the bulls got together. But it was decided imperative that one of us must give the alarm to our toiling men folks, now on the trail far below us, and hurry their arrival at the summit and place us out of danger. So I was judged fleet of foot and sound of lung, and having left dear Sissy on a high boulder in charge of the women, off I ran in terror, lest "Brigham" should overtake me, and when I gained an eminence from which I could look below in the valley, I could see our men folks on their toilsome march, and now was my chance to give the alarm. I straightened myself, filled my lungs to their fullest and forth went the cry, "Brigham's loose! Brigham's loose!" and the same time gesticulating with my arms. My voice rang out in clarion sounds, and at length was heard by the men below, though nothing could they tell of the cause for alarm, unless surely a band of savage Indians had surrounded us in our camp, and we should all be scalped ere they could reach us.

The men left their wagons on the trail, and for dear life they climbed the mountain to our rescue. But what was our chagrin, and mine in particular, when on the men reaching the camp everything was as quiet as the wilderness, cattle all lying down, and never a bull fight occurred. Oh, but the men were provoked at their hasty summons, and back they returned to their task on the trail. I was too mortified to endure the chaffing I received from all hands in the camp.

We reached a spot in the mountains where great snow banks lay, and on the 9th of July had a big game at snowballing.

Our trip with this party was the pleasantest. We took the "Johnson cut-off," coming out by Roopley's ranch, near Hangtown. We here slept the sleep of the just, I guess, under a spreading oak tree, and thus we passed our first night in California.

Dr. Pringree wished to hunt up some acquaintances in Hangtown, and invited William and I to accompany him on horseback into the mining town. We gladly accepted. I felt the importance of this, my first entrance into California, and naturally donned my most presentable apparel. This happened to be my black brocaded silk frock. Truly not a very suitable costume for horseback, but my wardrobe contained nothing preferable, so we three rode gaily into Hangtown, I a trifle in advance of my escorts. My horse seemed not inclined to wait for them, they having met an acquaintance and stopped for a few minutes. I felt the animal acting strangely, pawing the ground, and so forth, but still I sat firm in the saddle, when presto! down went the horse, rolling over on its side and landing me on the sidewalk, in front of a dry goods store. My companions hastened up to my rescue, and commented on my lack of skill in horsemanship, in thus allowing my horse to lie down in the saddle, though an overfeed of corn the previous night had caused the trouble. But I was a novice, and found my silk frock ruined with its contact on the horseback.

In a former letter I mentioned an English lady fellow-passenger on board a Missouri River boat, who was going to join her husband in California. I took a great fancy to her, and when we parted she made us promise to make her a visit if we ever came near her home, which happened to be near Hangtown. So now we enquired their location. It was at a small mining camp called White Rock, four miles from Hangtown. So out there we drove, and readily found our friend of the previous summer, Mrs. Hillhouse, who gave us a warm welcome, her husband being a well-to-do storekeeper. They wished us to remain at that place, and William obtained employment in "diggings" at $3.50 per day. We soon made acquaintances, and rented a room back of a little grocery, for which we paid $8 per month. The floor was dirt, and my bed a bunk in the wall. William slept on the floor in a buffalo robe and blankets. Through the cracks in the boards we could see the men in the grocery playing cards all night, and frequently when we awoke next morning the candle would be burning and the men still at cards.

We soon found it best to remove from this home, and decided to build us one. We engaged a carpenter, and our first California home was begun the day my baby was two years old, August 16, 1853. William hauled the lumber himself. We moved into the house in a week, soon as the frame was up. It was lined with dark calico, ceilings of muslin, four rooms and a pantry. So cozy we felt, and happy. We lived there over two years, during which time Mary was born, July 12, 1855. We then removed to Placerville, and I was engaged teaching private school and music.

William bought into a claim about this time, and we removed

to it on Weber creek, where we lived and I boarded his partners. Here Willie was born on January 22, 1857. The claim for a time paid wages, then the rains set in, creek raised, diggins gone, and we removed, made an unsuccessful attempt to return to the states, and finally went into Placer county from Sacramento City and joined a company in fluming the North Fork of the American River. Worked here a season, but it was a failure. It was at this place my little boy Willie ran into the river and was carried into the current, and must have drowned in my sight but for the providential appearance of a man on the opposite side of the river, who, hearing my shrieking, looked for the cause and saw my baby boy's head bobbing up and down on the water, and instantly went to his rescue.

I might continue this writing through all our early experiences of pioneer life, but as the journey Across the Plains was alone intended, it seems best to leave the record of after years, its trials and disappointments, for of each we have had full share. Still, I would here record that blessings unnumbered and unheeded have surrounded us in every path through which we have passed, and now I bring this journal to a close.

LUCY COOKE.

Virginia City, Nevada, July 30, 1895.

THE COMING TO AMERICA
OF TWO YOUNG ENGLISH GIRLS
IN THE YEAR 1848.

The following account of the journey to America of Lucy Rutledge and her sister, Marianne Rutledge, was copied from Lucy Cooke's note book by Genevieve Cooke, in March, 1912.

ON BOARD THE SHIP LONDON, BOUND FOR NEW York: Sailed from London August 11, 1848. Towed ten or twelve miles below Gravesend. In the course of the first day a quarrel took place between some of the steerage passengers, in consequence of one of the berths being let twice, and on the female going to claim it a man drew a knife at her. Complaint was immediately made to the pilot and first mate, when the latter with two gents went in search of the fellow in hiding to give him a hoist or a ducking. But he managed to escape the eyes of the searchers, consequently nothing more of the affair was heard.

The sky throughout the day was very cloudy. I had a very poor night's rest, but felt no regrets at leaving England.

Saturday, August 12. Was seasick, but felt better immediately. Nothing particular occurred throughout the day; the weather was very wet and the wind unfavorable.

Sunday, August 13. Rather fine morning. Went to the service in the saloon, where a clergyman read the prayers and Mr. May preached. The day was very wet. In the evening a scuffle took place with the carpenter, who knocked one of the second cabin passengers down for calling him one of the ship's servants. However, that passed over after having made me rather frightened for fear the carpenter (who had partaken rather freely of brandy) should do further mischief; but as soon as he went into his cabin he was locked in without a light.

Monday, August 14. Noon, very wet, arrived off Portsmouth at breakfast time. Wrote seven letters, then went on deck to see arrival of passengers. Some of the gents with the first pilot went in a boat to Portsmouth, as we were lying near two miles off. The captain, his lady and sister here came on board, and after taking on six sheep and barrels of water they drew up anchor and set sail. Passed around the Isle of Wight. Saw Brading, Ryde and Cowes very distinctly. The rain still continued to fall heavily. Between nine and ten at night the second pilot left us, but the wind still continued unfavorable.

Tuesday, August 15. A lovely day, though not very favorable for our vessel, the wind still contrary. In the morn we had a good game of shuffleboard. The awning was put up and all was very pleasant. In the evening dancing was commenced across deck; after that the Germans in the steerage sang most sweetly, but through jealousy the English steerage passengers, who were also singing, hissed the Germans.

Wednesday, August 16. Another lovely morning. I rose at half-past five o'clock, went out on deck soon after six. In the afternoon we came in sight of a fine vessel. She put up her colors and the captain and mate, after examining them some time and referring to a book, found that she was the *Adirondack,* bound for Havre from New York. We also showed our colors to let them know who we were. In the course of the afternoon a pilot boat made up to us (which is a very common occurrance) to see if they could get any letters to take ashore, which if they failed to do [here the record breaks off, as leaves have been lost.] (Passengers paid 6d. per letter for posting through pilot boats.)

Saturday, September 16, 1848. Arrived in New York, being five weeks and one day from the time we left London. Stayed at the United States Hotel until the morning of the 18th. Left on the six o'clock morning boat for Albany, where we arrived next morning at six. Breakfasted at the Delevan Hotel and left Albany by the half after seven o'clock train. Reached Utica at one o'clock, where we dined at Bagg's Hotel, then continued our journey in the car until within six miles of Auburn, when an accident occurred by an engine which was proceeding to [here the record ends, as leaves have been torn, but from memory Little Mother has given me the following]:

September 16, 1848. Soon after arriving at the United States Hotel she and her sister were alarmed by a loud and strange clamor; opened their door and ran into the hall to try to learn the cause. The "dreadful noise" seemed to be approaching, and they ran in the opposite direction in the hall, and with the noise growing louder and louder. They soon spied some one, and implored this individual to tell them what the trouble was that caused this dreadful clatter (they thinking it must be a fire or other danger). But they were quietly informed that it was the boy beating the gong for dinner. They had feared "judgment day had come."

Their first dinner in America afforded these two young English women and many of their fellow travelers some interest, and some amusement. There was a variety of edibles on the table, several of which were new to the travelers. Green corn was one. They eyed this strange vegetable, then watched other diners to try and find out in what way they should proceed to eat it. One diner was "stabbing at it" with his fork to try and pick it up, but gave up in despair. Later they observed a man pick it up, and holding it at each end of the cob between his fingers, began eating the kernels from it. This seemed "very strange" to the new comers. Here was where they first saw a rocking chair.

Following the accident mentioned, in which some cars were demolished and an engine wrecked and several passengers burned by escaping steam—one a blind woman—Little Mother has no record, and it is not clear in her memory as to how soon they proceeded on their trip across New York State on board one of the boats on the Erie Canal, though she cannot recall at what place they began their trip on the canal. They reached Buffalo in due time, however. She thinks they were two or more days traveling by canal boat. From Buffalo they went by lake steamer across Lakes Erie, Huron, and Michigan, in this roundabout way to Chicago. Met some very pleasant people on the lake boat. Cannot recall the name of the hotel at which they stayed in Chicago (which they pronounced "Chick-a-go"). They were bound for Rock Island, directly across the state of Illinois, on the Mississippi River.

A fellow traveler at the same hotel, Mr. Hamilton, was also going to Rock Island, and as they would have to drive across the state they decided to engage a driver with double team to take them on this journey, which lasted several days. Mr. Hamilton was an attorney. He was en route to Wisconsin, and proved a very congenial guide. In an account given by Little Mother she states:

On our arrival at Rock Island we stopped at a hotel. Everything seemed strange to us. We saw little children who lived at the hotel running about barefooted. At the same time noticed one little girl with a ring on her finger. This astonished me, as it seemed that it was not through poverty, as I had always in London known it to be that a child went barefooted. Much that to my sister and myself seemed novel in this new world our traveling companion explained as the customs of the country in which we had now decided to make our home.

We crossed the Mississippi River by ferry boat to Davenport, then a rising city, and there hired a conveyance to take us up the river to Le Claire, to our Uncle's home (Mr. Rutledge), a distance of about sixteen miles. Mr. Hamilton, presumably having become interested in "the two English girls," asked to be allowed to bear us company to our uncle's home, as our destination was still on his route to Wisconsin, and he was desirous of seeing us safely to our journey's end and welcomed by our Uncle Rutledge.

This was on Saturday, and at about eight o'clock in the evening we reached LeClaire, and on inquiry found that Uncle lived a short distance beyond, at a little settlement called Parkhurst. Our hearts doubtless throbbed with excitement as we were now so near our journey's end, and the surroundings were getting narrowed down to a very primitive form of living. We stopped one or two passengers and inquired for Mr. Rutledge, or Elder Rutledge, as he was called, being a minister of Baptist persuasion and stationed over a small church at Le Claire.

We soon found his dwelling, a little, unpretentious affair, more so than our faintest imagery pictured. A one-room cabin located on the bank of the Mississippi! Why had Uncle persuaded us to come to him, to take that long and expensive journey, and find him and his family all crowded into a one-roomed cabin, and apparently his circumstances in keeping with his house!

We alighted from our vehicle, paid our driver, and were soon receiving the welcome of our Aunt and three or four cousins whom we had last seen in England a few years before. Uncle was absent in Le Claire on our arrival, but soon returned, as he was expecting us, we having sent him word from New York. After our greetings were over, I began to feel some chagrin that we had been ushered into such a room, as it seemed crowded with two double beds, a cook stove and other accessories of domesticity, and with Mr. Hamilton, a stranger. I felt that we should have been shown into the parlor, or best room, and thus give Mr. Hamilton some idea of the surroundings we were to have in our adopted home. I saw a door in the farther side of the room, and I inquired of one of my cousins as to where it lead, thinking, of course, that it opened into another room. My cousin answered me by opening the door and showing me the buttery, lined with shelves covered with dishes and all household belongings! I looked at the girl, and asked, "Have you but one room?" "Yes." Well, our mortification and disappointment knew no bounds. Had we left a comfortable home in London and traveled all this distance to find ourselves placed in such surroundings!

Mr. Hamilton soon bade us good night, but he remained a short time in the vicinity of Uncle's, doubtless to see how we adapted ourselves to our new surroundings, for he was becoming interested in his traveling companions. It was not long before Sister and I upbraided our dear Uncle for his seeming unkindness or want of prudence in having persuaded us to come to this strange country to "rough it," as was the rule with the majority.

The first night of our sojourn, Uncle kindly gave up his share of one bed to our needs, and he found sleeping quarters at a neighbor's, and thus we lay down in disgust and tears at our uncomfortable and unlooked-for surroundings.

Mr. Hamilton soon realized our disappointment, and sympathized with us. He would gladly have rendered us any assistance in making our new home more satisfactory. But we were our Uncle's guests, and with him and his family we must make the best of the situation. And so Mr. Hamilton had to leave us and continue his journey up the river, promising to stop over on his return and see how we were becoming reconciled. We embraced in a farewell, but we never met again.

Although they "never met again," here is a copy of a letter from Mr. Hamilton, addressed to Lucy Rutledge, Rockingham, Iowa, dated October 5, 1850, nearly a year after she had become

Mrs. Lucy Rutledge Cooke, indicating that the writer had preserved a warm memory of "the two English girls."

Miss Rutledge—Dear Friend: I am again in the bright clime of the West—the free, the joyous, the glorious West. I love this odorous clime—the brightness of its skies—the vastness of its plains—the bloom of its flowers—and the song of its birds.

I remember some who live here—would joy to meet them—thou are one of them.

I am en route for Minnesota; leave on the "Menominee" in a few moments.

If you will favor me with your address, I will try and do myself the pleasure of visiting you, if agreeable, on my return down the river next week.

Please write me at Dubuque, Iowa.

Very truly,
H.H. Hamilton.

Galena, August 5, 1850.

Our disgust at everything seemed rather to increase, and the cooped-up quarters of the family were a continual annoyance. We did little but wander about out of doors, and weep and bemoan our situation. My dear Uncle did all in his power to reconcile us, though at times wordy warfare was all the satisfaction he gained from us. He rented a room at a neighbor's for our sleeping accommodation, and there he tried to arrange for our comfort for the winter, it being now October. He bought a warming stove, a rag carpet, bedstead and chairs, and these, with our packing cases and contents, i.e., curtains, bed clothing, etc., soon made a cozy room for us, and we quite looked forward to the evening's coming, that we might trudge down the hill to our lodgings. The winter came on and was very severe. The Mississippi River was frozen hard all over, and teams were hauling across daily. We had among our possessions a tin water bottle, for in those days rubber ones were not thought of. We filled this tin bottle for a foot-warmer one night as usual, but unfortunately the cap was not screwed tightly, and in the morning we found it had leaked and the water had frozen at the foot of the bed, and the sheets were frozen stiff together at our feet.

The family in whose home we had our room seemed never to tire of watching us, and our packing cases were regarded as containing treasures unheard of in those regions, as we were known to be just from London.

I remember how a little girl came peeping in at our door on Christmas morning, and with a sly glance at us exclaimed: "Christmas gift! Christmas gift!" We, not realizing her meaning, allowed her to repeat it several times, and then we replied: "Yes, where is it?" On telling our Uncle, he explained that this was the custom on Christmas morn in America, and that the little girl expected us to make her a gift from our store of treasures.

As time passed and we began to make acquaintances, we found our surroundings more congenial than at first appeared. The people though nearly all poorly dressed, were generally well educated and pleasant. The women seemed to regard our clothing as the newest style and most desirable of adoption. We seldom went out but we were watched at all points, and then would come requests from one and another for the loan of this or that garment for taking of pattern. This was a source of much annoyance to us the whole of the winter.

My Uncle was having a church built for his followers, and this was in course of construction when we arrived. As soon as the roof was on services were held, and of course we had to attend. I remember that the seats were boards, supported at each end by blocks of wood. The ceiling was not yet finished, and a flock of pigeons were roosting in the rafters, and much to our astonishment and amusement a man got a long pole and went about shoving the feathered occupants away before the congregation could be seated for service. This was our first attendance at church in America. Our presence seemed to be of more interest than the service. While living at my Uncle's ("Elder Rutledge's") we were known as "the Elder's two nieces from London."

Soon after Christmas Uncle suggested that I open a little private school, and he engaged a room in the house adjoining that in which we were lodging, and belonging to Mr. Ames, whose daughter always importuned me for the loan of my garments from which to take the pattern. This always annoyed me. In the house beyond that in which I opened my school a family by the name of Cody lived, one son being later known to fame as Colonel Cody, or "Buffalo Bill."

I asked as tuition for each pupil $2.50 a quarter. I had some eight or ten pupils, and at the end of the quarter my patrons desired to pay me in produce, cash, it seemed, being unobtainable except just following harvest time. One patron offered me a load of bricks as tuition for his child, he owning a brick yard. In consternation I appealed to Uncle, who said he would take the bricks and pay me the cash, as he desired to enlarge his house, and could use the bricks. Other patrons gave me orders on the general merchandise store, sixteen miles distant. But as I was well supplied with clothing which I brought from London, and had no use for groceries, I was not inspired to continue my school another quarter.

Meanwhile, my sister had married and gone to live on a farm near Rockingham, Scott County, Iowa, and she and her husband, Mr. Willis, invited me to make my home with them and start a school there. This I did. Mr. Willis very kindly built a little house on his farm, and I had some twelve or sixteen pupils, who came from near and far.

Singing schools were in vogue then, and every little church had its own singing school for the young people. Many of my evenings were spent in this pastime. Young men would call for me, and to the merry jingle of sleigh bells we would cross the Mississippi River on the ice in our sleighs, and rolled up in great buffalo robes the merry parties would arrive at the little church in Port Byron, where a happy evening would be spent.

Here again I carried on my little school for a quarter, during which time I had frequently heard of an English lady in Moline, Illinois, who came over regularly and was teaching music, both vocal and instrumental, in Davenport, Iowa. I was most anxious to meet her and so through a friend, Mrs. Telfare, whose daughter was receiving instructions under this lady, Mrs. Sarah Cooke, I was invited to spend an afternoon at her home and make Mrs. Cooke's acquaintance. Davenport was but four miles from my brother-in-law's home in Rockingham. I happily accepted this invitation. Mrs. Cooke and I were mutually attracted to each other, and I was invited to visit her at her home in Moline, the following week, and I almost counted the hours to the time set. Here Mrs. Cooke was very pleasantly situated, though what appealed to me the most in her pleasant home was the piano. There were several other English ladies present, and I was asked to play. I sat down to the instrument and began to play, but the memories of home and surroundings where I last sat down to such an instrument crowded up into my thoughts so strongly that my emotion was not to be controlled, and I burst into tears. The guests all realized the state of my feelings, but urged me to play on, and I did so for a short time. Then Mrs. Cooke kindly took my place and entertained the guests. This was indeed a red letter day to me. Toward evening we returned to the Iowa side of the Mississippi, ferrying across. I returned to the farm in Rockingham, happy in the thoughts of my new acquaintances and friends.

A few weeks later Mrs. Cooke came over to Rockingham to call on me, having ferried across the river with her span of spirited horses, driven by her eldest son, William, whom I had not previously met. They dined and spent the afternoon with us. Mrs. Cooke was desirous that I return with them and make her a visit, which invitation I accepted with anticipation of a happy two weeks.

During this visit I met Mrs. Hasbrook, another English lady, who conducted a private school in Moline. Mrs. Hasbrook showed interest in me and later asked me to become her assistant, which request I was glad to comply with, and it was arranged between Mrs. Cooke and myself for me to continue at her home as a boarder. This was in the spring of 1849. I enjoyed my work at Mrs. Hasbrook's school very much. Meantime a close friendship was springing up between young Mr. Cooke and myself, and on December 26th of that year we were married. The wedding took place at the home of Mr. and Mrs. Yarwood, friends of Mrs. Cooke's, in Davenport, the Rev. Mr. Louderback, Episcopal minister, officiating.

Our wedding taking place in the middle of a school quarter, I returned in January, after the holidays, to finish my term. Soon after this I came down with "chills and fever," then prevalent in that section, which lasted some months. Meantime, while I was finishing out my school term, we were planning to move to Dubuque, Iowa. Mrs. Cooke, Sr., established herself there, and resumed the teaching of music, Mr. Cooke, Sr. remaining with William and myself in Moline until the spring of 1851. We then joined Mrs. Cooke and settled in Dubuque.

GRANDMA'S RHYMES.
WISE AND OTHERWISE.

The following rhymes were written by Lucy Cooke
after she had been stricken with blindness.

AN ACROSTIC
140 Fern Avenue, San Francisco, Sunday, May 2, 1903.

Gentle maiden, daughter mine,
   Engrossed with cares of life;
Now would I wish those cares resigned,
   Except for those of wife.
Valued thy skill, as proven oft,
   In giving ease for pain.
Each day attributes to thy worth when
   Vanished health returns to bless, and
Eyes shine bright again.

AN ACROSTIC
Towle, Placer County, Summer of 1902.

Just now at eventide,
On Sarah's porch I'm sitting
Enjoying thoughts of thee.
Endeared by holiest ties.
Could we but dwell together,
Or in the same pathway tread,
Oft lovingly your hand would lead,
Knowing to me the way was dark,
Except as lit by love.

CROSSING THE PLAINS IN 1852
COUNTRY SOUNDS
Towle, May, 1901.

A bright, sunny morn there comes now to greet,
  In place of the constant rain;
So I'll hie me away to my favorite seat
  And list for sweet sounds again.
There's the song of the bird in the pine tree near,
  As he sings to his listening mate,
And the low, sweet sound of a bird near the ground—
  I hear it both early and late.

And other sounds than songs of birds,
    There come to my listening ear;
The donkey's bray, on the hills away,
    And clarion's voice so clear.
And the grasshopper's click, with its limbs so quick,
    And cricket 'neath the sod,
These all give their praise, tho' in different ways,
    To their one Great Maker—God.
Another sound now strikes my ear,
    I listen to its call;
The buzz saw at the planing mill—
    Most useful sound of all.
For there our men and mother's boys
    Do daily earn their bread,
And thus while some are loitering,
    The loved at home are fed.
There're sounds of twinkling bells I hear
    Along the country road.
Of sweet breath'd kine as driven on
    By horseman or the goad.
And bands of sheep, with lambs that bleat,
    All seeking pastures green,
As patiently they move along—
    Could aught more charm, I we'en?
Just now a bell in measured tone
    Proclaims the schoolhouse near.
And children shout for joy let out
    With voices loud and clear.
The hour is noon—say not too soon—
    An aching void comes o'er me;
But hark! a dear, familiar voice
    To dinner now it calls me.

121

Lucy Rutledge Cooke

THE OLD ARM CHAIR
Towle, 1902.

The old arm chair, not the one in the song,
That a grandmother sat in for years so long,
But the one on the porch at Sarah's home,
That always stood ready, whoever might come.
This chair was of oak, though in style rather crude,
Could boast not of lathe nor skilled turner's mood.
It first found its use in cabin at mill,
And but for our boys would have been there still,
In summer a woodbine, both thrifty and tall,
Would give by its shade a kind welcome to all.
In winter, when leaves were all gone from the trees,
Still a seat in this chair would oftentimes please.
But summer or winter, ah, little to me,
Since changes of seasons I no longer see.
So I sit and I listen to sounds in the air,
Or sing to the praise of this old arm chair.

A SUMMER OUTING
Lines written while visiting at Joe's, the Flournoy Ranch,
in Genesee Valley, Plumas County, in August, 1903.

Shall I tell of an outing this season I've had,
   To dear Joe and his kindly wife?
With their dear little babe, scarce a twelve-month old,
   Each adding their pleasure to life.

T'was way up to Plumas my footsteps were led,
  Where the air is so balmy and fine,
Each breath was a pleasure and mine without measure,
  So filled with the fragrance of pine.
Each day by the hour in hammock I swung,
  And then I would listen for sounds;
The bluejay's call, or squirrel or quail,
Or cackling hens, or stage with mail,
  Where letters from loved ones were found.
Sometimes through the clover I wandered with Joe—
  Through the garden or orchard so fair;
I would feel of the fruit-laden boughs o'er my head
Breathe a sigh from my heart, though nothing were said,
  For the shadow must ever be there.
Then a change of the program, dear Joe he would come,
  And lovingly lead me to dinner;
Here "Father" and Will and mother and babe,
With Indian Rosy as helping maid,
  Each doing their best as bread-winner.
Fried chicken or grouse, or oftentimes quail,
  Deliciously cooked to a turn,
Let's praise the dear girl who is chef at that house,
  And may she have "money to burn."
And when the day's over, and the work is all done,
  Dear Joe with his baby and wife,
With rest of the household—some six, eight or ten—
  Adjourn to the porch without strife.
Some talk of the weather, their work, or the farm,
  And some of the long, long ago,
But bedtime approaching, they call for a song
  From my boy, with his pleasing banjo.

AN ACROSTIC
1902

Gently as twilight settles
O'er mountain top and hill,
Deep'ning as night approaches, and
Stars their azure fill.
Alone, yet not alone,
Comrades and friends lie here,
Resting from all earth's labors,
Embittered by no tear.

A TALE OF KITTENS
Towle, Placer County

Oh, Genevieve, dear Genevieve, say don't you want a kitten?
   That friend who takes one off our hands,
   Transporting safe to other lands,
Will never "get the mitten."
Your Auntie's life is bothered much with dogs and cats galore,
That wait for meat or cry for milk about the kitchen door.
Last Monday it was washing day, the clothes were lying round;
A busy pup got in his work, and with them strewed the ground.
Your Aunty says the kits must drown, tied in a sack together;
Not one of us will do the deed—what, drown those kittens, never!
The other day she asked a boy, would he with kittens go?
He turned aside, then shook his head, and firmly answered "No."
So kits still live, and yet may grow to useful mother cats,
And learn to "earn their board and keep," and scare away the rats.

A MIDNIGHT REVERIE
Towle, 1902

Oh, the croaking of the frogs,
And bark of moonstruck dogs,
And cricket's constant whir-r-r—
All nature seems astir.
    Whilst I
Lie here so still and ponder,
O'er this and that and yonder,
And wonder why the fates
Securely close the gates
    To Slumberland.
If this the cross intended,
Lord, give me strength to bear,
That when the task is ended
I then the crown shall wear.

Mary, that name most illustrious
Among all the fair daughters of men;
Royal ladies from birth have oft borne it,
Yet others of lowlier mien.

Written in San Francisco, August 23, 1914.

There's a spot on the hillside,
  So near the old home,
Where our loved ones
  We lay down to rest
No spot more befitting
  The old pioneer or the son
On the slope they knew best.

Each morn the bright sun
  Gilds the treetops with gold,
Free birds flitter round on the wing;
  The hum of wing'd insects
Is heard all around,
  While zephyrs a requiem sing.

  Years forty-nine,
  In rain and sunshine,
Together life's pathway we pressed.
Here I would lie
  Side by side with the one
Who in life was the dearest and best.

THE VOICE OF GRANDMA
Lines written by "Sister" Stone, March, 1912, to "Little Mother."

In the golden glow of morning,
  'Ere yet full day's begun,
And sparrows on the housetops
  Are welcoming in the sun;
From the little bed in the corner,
  Flanked by the old arm chair,
    "Mary, are you there?
    Mary, where's Mary?"
I hear the voice of Grandma—

Waiting—listening—ever listening—
  She sits with list'ning ear,
All through her days of darkness,
  For voice and step so dear;
Of her whose hand is ready
  To smooth away her care.
And so Grandma keeps calling—
    "Mary, where's Mary?
    Mary, are you there?"

And when the cold waters of the Jordan
  Press close to the faltering feet,
With hands outstretched to the Master
  To lead to the Golden Street,
As sweet celestial music
  Bursts on her enraptured ear,
Again the first call of Grandma—
    "Mary, where's Mary?"
    Mary, are you here?"

The darkness is gone forever,
    Gone for aye the night,
But still as she looks around her,
    Mid sounds of Heaven's delight,
And as triumphant chorus
    Greets her entranced ear,
She'll say again, "My Mary,
      Oh, Mary are you here?"

And some sweet day in the future—
    In time not counted by men,
As paeans of heavenly music
    Proclaim a freed soul—then
Grandma—still watching—listening—
For the voice that yet is dear,
    Cries for the last time,
"Mary, Mary, are you here?"
    And with rapturous joy hears answer—
"Yes, Ma,—safe home, I'm here."

Grandma lost her sight in the latter part of July, 1900, and was totally blind to her death in 1915.

GENEVIEVE COOKE VISITS LONDON SCENES
OF LUCY RUTLEDGE'S GIRLHOOD DAYS.

In the summer of 1907 Genevieve Cooke had opportunity to visit London, England, the birthplace of Lucy Rutledge, and the following letter from her to Grandma Cooke may well find a place in these pages:

No. 10 Coliseum Terrace, Albany St.,
London, England, July 3, 1907.

WELL, MY MUMSIE DARLING:
Here I am in great, big, old London. I arrived at Victoria Station about 7:30 Monday evening, after an interesting trip from Cologne. Rain fell all through the part on the continent, but it was clear crossing from Calais, and the steamer cut through the water like a swift greyhound. It was rather rough, but I enjoyed it, and I loved the scenery from Dover to London. Tell Mr. Shinn I saw many beautiful hopfields en route.

Tuesday morning I started out betimes. I carried your map folded at the section I wanted, and I wandered along Albany street across New Road into Portland road, and along Great Portland street to Oxford street. I enjoyed the walk and nosing about in Oxford street. I took a bus for the bank (climbed to the top and enjoyed the trip from this high perch).

I took luncheon away down in Theadneedle street, at Slater's, a very nice restaurant, with numerous branches in different parts of London. After luncheon I again mounted to the top of a bus for another long ride, past the statue of Wellington, away down town, rode out along Cheapside and around St. Paul's to Fleet street. Then on to the Strand and along Haymarket and Piccadilly to Berkeley street. The "cabbie" called it "Barkley" street. I walked up "Barkley" street to "Barkley" Square, along Mount street to South Audley street, and on to Grosvenor Square, which by the way is a circle and not a square bit of park. Just here I met little Lucy Rutledge with a skipping rope. We took a fancy to each other and decided to trudge about the neighborhood together. We thought we would go into Grosvenor Square and sit and chat for a time, but there is a high iron fence which circles it, and we found the gates locked. A number of hackney cabs stand at this square, and I asked a cabbie if there was no way of going into the square. "Oh, no, Miss," he said; "only the people in the fine 'ouses about the square 'ave keys and go in there. It is not for the public." Lucy and I were both disappointed, for she told me she used to run in there. (This Mumsie says I am mistaken in, as she only played about the square—was never inside.—G.C.)

So we wandered hand in hand down Grosvenor street to Avery row—a tiny street running from Grosvenor street to Brook street—a queer little street, which Lucy said had changed very much since she was there before. We walked along to No. 7, which is a small tailor shop. We opened the door and walked in. The tailor is a pleasant little man, and we stopped and had a chat with him, and promised to send him a suit to clean and press.

We then walked on through to Brook street. Little Lucy Rutledge said she was glad she did not have to live in Avery row now, but we are going back to see the little tailor again, and call on Mr. Drew, Mr. Baker, Mr. Powell and Mr. Beattie along the way.

We wanted to wave from an upstairs window in No. 7 to a little boy in a nearby yard, but Lucy said he had moved away. The house at No. 7 is a low three-story, cement I think, painted a pale yellow. We wandered down Brook street, and came right upon the steps of St. George's, Hanover Square. We were so pleased to find this old church. It did not look so big as we thought it would, but the columns are huge. Three children were playing on the steps, two little girls and a baby about three years. Lucy and I circled our arms about the columns, for Lucy said she always did this and loved to run around them. Pigeons were billing and cooing in the eaves and have their homes there.

From here we decided to go to St. George's Chapel burying grounds, as Lucy said her parents were buried there. We thought we would walk, as we so enjoyed gazing into the shops, and we did not mind the distance. We went through Maddox street to Regents street, and into Oxford street, and trudged along, enjoying every block. We stopped at a little dairy luncheon place, opposite Park street, and had a cup of chocolate and some pastry, then continued our walk to St. George's chapel.

The old chapel is still there, with its many tablets on the walls to departed parishioners, who are there enclosed. These tablets have interesting, and sometimes amusing, lines to the memory of the departed. The chapel, however, is otherwise vacant. There are no chairs or benches to hide the time-worn stone floor. But joining it and practically enclosing it is a newer building—brick—called the Chapel of the Ascension. This is open all day, and invites the passer-by to enter and rest. Lucy and I walked in and found paper-covered books on a small table, giving the history of the new chapel. I bought one for Lucy at a shilling. We enquired of the little Englishman who sat at the table if we might wander into the burial ground. "Oh, yes," he said; it is now a public playground, though still fenced in." We inquired about the graves of Lucy's but we enjoyed very much wandering through together and seeing the things that had been there since long before Lucy was born. Hundreds of pigeons roost and nest in the cornices on the outside of the museum, and coo, coo, constantly.

On my return yesterday I found cards of Dr. and Mrs. Bedford Fenwick and Mrs. Breay, who called in the afternoon.

Well, Mumsie Darling, I must bring this epistle to a close. I love London, and will write you again soon. Isn't it nice that I met little Lucy Rutledge here to show me about?

Much love to all, and wishing you were all enjoying this with me.

GENEVIEVE.

The following tribute to "Mother" appeared in the Healdsburg Tribune, *October 28, 1915:*

IN MEMORIAM — MOTHER

AT REST—In San Franciso, October 22, 1915, Lucy Rutledge Cooke, aged 88 years, 7 months and 12 days; a native of London, England; mother of Mrs. A. Lane of Reno; Mrs. W.G. Thompson of San Francisco; W.R. Cooke of Orosi; F.W. Cooke of Healdsburg; Genevieve Cooke of San Francisco; J.E. Cooke of Taylorville, Plumas County; Mrs. G. W. Hatch of Oakland and the late Henry S. Cooke of Virginia City, Nevada.

There were tears, of course, as we stood at the coffin and looked down on the face of the dead. But the tears were not those of grief that was beyond comfort; they were not the evidence of sorrow that tried our souls—of mourning that was without hope. For in our hearts, beneath the tears that would not check, we knew the eyes that for long, long years had been sightless had now been opened by the Master's touch, that the dear old soul now looked upon her Pilot face to face.

Peace, and tranquility of soul, and abiding faith were written in every lineament of the countenance. And beneath our outward sorrow, softening the pain of an eternal parting, our hearts were glad in the knowledge that the years of our mother had been long, and that she went to her endless rest as a child to its mother's arms at close of day—a-weary.

Born in the world's greatest city, Lucy Rutledge grew to womanhood in an environment of shops, and congested streets, and cabbies, of restricted scope for childhood's pleasures. At ten years of age she was one of the vast throng that lined the streets of London to look upon the young Queen Victoria as she passed in the coronal procession, and the memory of that incident remained through life.

It was a long step from the busy streets of London to the wagon of the emigrant train bound across the plains to the gold fields of California, but the young English woman faltered not at following her husband on that hazardous journey.

And in the mines of California and Nevada for fifty years, this London-bred woman gave of her talents of mind and voice to the communities—the little mining camps and towns—of which she was at times a part.

Ever before the sons and daughters of her home she held ideals that stimulated ambition; always she pointed the path of right and truth, of loyalty to home and country. From cover to cover her Bible was an open book—a daily counselor, the strength and comfort of the long years of her blindness.

She was nearly ninety when the call to eternal rest came, yet her heart retained its youth, and age could not take from her the joy of living, planning, learning, hoping. At eighty-seven she exclaimed: "Oh, if I but had my sight, I feel that I could set the world on fire!"

But in the last weeks her life was a dream; fitful and broken, it may be, yet permitting her to live again the pioneer days: "Aren't we almost there?" she sighed. "It seems such a long, long way."

Yes, she is there now, I know.

And I feel that I have much to be grateful for that she was my mother:

I am grateful for the sound physical bodies that she bequeathed to her children; for the religious training that she administered in our youth; for the happiness that came into the days of my boyhood through the kindness of her heart; for the love and content and concord that held an abiding place in the home in which she ruled; for the inspiration she presented to attain to full stature of manhood and womanhood; and for the example of ambition, faith and optimism that gave to her the freshness and mental vitality of youth through all the long, long years of her life.

May her every hope and fullest faith be justified.

The following tribute to Mother appeared in the "By the Way" column of the Healdsburg Tribune June 4, 1914:

ON A RECENT VISIT TO SAN FRANCISCO, I SPENT A short while at the home of a white-haired old lady—blind these many years. But though the light of her eyes has been extinguished, and unending earthly darkness has enveloped her, this old lady shows marvelous interest in the world's activities of today, and her mind is alive with plans and hopes for the future.

"Oh, if I just had my sight, I feel I could set the world on fire!"

And if I could put into type the emphasis and vigor with which this declaration was made, I believe you would agree with me that she holds a marvelous grip on life and its opportunities.

How old, do you ask, is this white haired lady?

Well, she is not sensitive on this score, so it will not wound her feelings, I know, to say that the days of her life run back to the opening of the second quarter of last century—March 1827, to be specific, and that totals up to eighty-seven years.

And more than sixty years of that long life have been spent here in the West—in the mining camps and towns of California and Nevada.

137

This state of ours has grown and prospered to a wonderful degree since she came within its borders, away back in 1853. And in that growth and development she has had a part—that is, if the rearing of a family of eight sons and daughters to an honorable and useful manhood and womanhood counts for anything in the making of a commonwealth.

Yes, hers has been an active, fruitful life, her early years combining the vocations of school teacher and music instructor, and while she was resting, in between classes and music pupils, she cared for her home ones, and in the long winter evenings up in the little mining town in the Sierras which was for a quarter of a century her home, she found time to read aloud from book or story-paper to the growing family about her, or to tell of her girlhood years in the great city of London, or of the trials and incidents of the journey by emigrant wagon across the plains.

A life of achievement such as this, it would seem, ought to justify this great-grandmother in folding her hands and calmly awaiting, in peace and comfort and with tranquil soul, life's closing hour.

But here is this white-haired old lady, helpless in her sightlessness, with a retrospective vision taking in the scenes on London's streets at the coronation of Queen Victoria, the long and arduous journey across the plains to the goldfields of California, and many years of the vicissitudes and hardships, successes and failures, in the mining camps—here is this old lady today, with ambition and desire to ''set the world on fire.''

In the light of this example, what measure of excuse have we youngsters of fifty, sixty and seventy years of age to think of losing our grip on life's activities, of dropping to the rear in the marching hosts that are grappling and besting the existence problems of this twentieth century.

Yes, his old lady, rising close to the century mark, blind though she is, has a marvelous conception of life, a wonderful willingness and desire to yet have a part in the world's progress.

But perhaps my judgment is warped, perhaps my vision magnifies and lends unreality to the record of the long service that has been hers, perhaps my eyes do not see clearly through the mists that arise as I contemplate her life, because—well, because—she is my mother.

Index

COLOPHON

The *Lucy Rutledge Cooke,* CROSSING THE PLAINS IN 1852 *was printed in the workshop of Glen Adams, which is located in the quiet country village of Fairfield, southern Spokane County in Washington state and one township removed from the Idaho line. Basic book design was by Dale La Tendresse, who also set the book in type, using a Model 7300 Editwriter computer photosetter. The typeface used is 14 on 17 Garamond with page numbers and running heads in 14 point Mahogany. Camera-darkroom work was by Sylvia Fenich using a 660C DS (Japanese) camera and a LogE automatic film developing machine. The sheets were printed by Dave Hooper using a 28-inch Heidelberg press, model KORS. Paper stock is seventy-pound Island Offset. Folding was by Garry Adams using a 22x28 Baum folding machine. Assembly was by Bonnie Cozzetto. This was a fun project. We had no special difficulty with the work.*